RISE AND SHINE MORNING GLORY

Time to Get Shit Done

Copyright 2023 Stephen Cartledge

All rights reserved. No part of this book may be reproduced, stored in a retrieval system, or transmitted in any form or by any means - whether electronic, mechanical, photocopying, recording, or otherwise - without prior written permission from the copyright holder, except for brief quotations incorporated in critical reviews and certain other noncommercial uses permitted by copyright law.

This book contains original content created with the assistance of AI technology. While the content was generated with the help of an AI assistant, it should be noted that it was not AI generated. The AI assistant served as a tool to enhance and facilitate the creative process but did not solely generate the content. The author's ideas, insights, and creative contributions remain integral to the work.

The use of AI technology, in this case, was intended to aid in research, organization, and augmentation of the author's creative process. The resulting content is the result of a collaboration between the author and the AI assistant, combining human ingenuity and technological support to bring this book to life.

Any similarities between the content of this book and other works are purely coincidental. The views and opinions expressed in this book are those of the author and do not necessarily reflect the views or opinions of the AI assistant used in its creation.

Unauthorized copying, distribution, or use of any part of this book, whether in physical or digital form, is strictly prohibited and may be subject to legal action.

stepheninfo9@gmail.com
Date of publication :- 27/11/2023
Printed by Amazon

ISBN : 9798863240657

Join our facebook community @ Rise And Shine Morning Glory.

Disclaimer

Disclaimer: The following statement serves as a friendly reminder before you delve into the pages of "Rise and Shine Morning Glory".

Dear reader, please note that the contents of this book are intended to inspire and guide you on your journey towards a more balanced and fulfilling life. However, remember that every individual is unique, and what works for one person may not be the perfect fit for another.

Throughout these pages, valuable strategies and insights will be shared to help you eliminate chaos, create a powerful routine, and find joy in each moment. However, it is essential to approach these recommendations with an open mind and tailor them to your own circumstances and preferences.

Any activities or strategies described in "Rise And Shine Morning Glory" should be conducted at your own risk. The author and publisher are not responsible for any accidents, injuries, or negative consequences that may result from the implementation of these activities. It is crucial to exercise caution.

Keep in mind that achieving balance and infusing positivity into your routine requires dedication, experimentation, and self-discovery. The journey may not always be smooth, but it is the process of growth and the small victories along the way that truly matter.

Lastly, while this book aims to provide guidance and support, it is important to remember that personal responsibility plays a significant role in implementing any lifestyle changes. Always consult a qualified professional when needed and listen to your own intuition as you embark on your unique path towards happiness and self-improvement.

Author's Dedication:

This book is dedicated to my beloved daughter Vanessa Jean Cartledge, my wonderful son Jack Cartledge, and my loving wife Boonyarat Cartledge. Fon, your unwavering support, love, and encouragement have been the driving force behind the creation of this book. Your presence in my life has inspired me to pursue my passions and strive for personal growth. I am forever grateful for your presence and the joy you bring to my world. May this book serve as a reminder of the love and appreciation I have for each of you.

A Note to the Reader:

Welcome! Thank you for picking up "Rise And Shine Morning Glory". This book is designed to bring a positive transformation to your mornings, with the ultimate goal of changing your entire life for the better. However, it is important to keep in mind that personal growth and transformation require consistent effort and dedication.

While "Rise And Shine Morning Glory" offers strategies and activities that have the potential to revolutionize your morning routines, it is vital to remember that results may vary from person to person. Each individual has a unique set of circumstances, goals, and challenges. What might work wonders for one person may not have the same impact for another.

It is essential to approach this book with an open mind and a willingness to adapt the ideas presented to suit your specific needs. Experiment, take what resonates with you, and leave what doesn't. Routines and strategies should be personalized to align with your goals, values, and lifestyle.

It is also crucial to balance your enthusiasm for change with self-care and self-compassion. Remember that change takes time and it's okay to stumble along the way. Embrace the process, be patient with yourself, and acknowledge the progress you make, no matter how small.

Lastly, always prioritize your well-being and safety when implementing new activities or making changes to your routines. Consult with professionals or experts if you have any concerns or questions about the applicability or safety of specific strategies.

Thank you for embarking on this journey with "Morning Game Changer." May it truly be a life-changing experience for you, shaping your mornings into a springboard for a fulfilling and joyful life.

Be part of our facebook group . morning glory community

A morning routine poem - by Stephen Cartledge

In the land of dawn's first light, where dreams awake,
A morning ritual, a routine I make,
For in these moments, as the sun does rise,
Lies the key to unlock life's precious prize.

With eyes still heavy, I rise from my slumber,
Embracing the day, its wonders to uncover,
For a morning routine, it sets the stage,
Guiding my steps on life's vibrant page.

I stretch my limbs, like a tree reaching high,
Inviting energy, banishing the sigh,
For in each movement, I find my strength,
Preparing my body, for life's entire length.

I cleanse my mind, with meditative breaths,
Releasing the worries, the struggles, the depths,
For in this silence, I find my peace,
A moment to let go, and let my worries cease.

I nourish my body, with wholesome fare,
Fruits and grains, a nutritious affair,
For in each bite, I fuel my soul,
Giving me the energy to reach my goal.
I set my intentions, with words of grace,

Affirming my purpose, at my own pace,
For in these affirmations, I find my drive,
A compass to guide me, as I strive.

With each tick of the clock, my morning unfolds,
A symphony of tasks, a story yet untold,
For in this routine, I find my rhythm,
A melody of life, a daily anthem.

For a morning routine, it's more than a chore,
It sets the tone for what lies in store,
For in these moments, I claim my day,
With purpose and passion, I find my way.

So let us embrace the importance, my friend,
Of a morning routine that has no end,
For in these rituals, we find our worth,
Nurturing our souls, right here on Earth.

Chapters

1. Embracing Change: A Mindset Shift
2. Decluttering Your Environment for Mental Clarity
3. Setting Clear and Achievable Goals
4. Designing Your Ideal Morning Routine
5. The Power of Prioritization: Focus on What Matters
6. Developing Effective Time Management Strategies
7. Overcoming Procrastination: Taking Action Now
8. Harnessing the Power of Habits for Productivity
9. Mastering Digital Distractions
10. Balancing Work and Personal Life: Creating Boundaries
11. The Art of Saying No: Setting Healthy Boundaries
12. Nurturing Self-Care and Wellness in Your Routine
13. Igniting Passion and Finding Purpose
14. Cultivating a Positive Mindset for Success
15. Owning Your Time: Creating a Weekly Review Process
16. Sustaining Motivation: Momentum for the Long Run.

A note from the author

Acknowledgements

About the author

CHAPTER 1. EMBRACING CHANGE: A MINDSET SHIFT

Let's start with this question.
If change is the nature of life, both personal and organizational, then why is it our nature to resist change so vigorously?

Ah, the paradox of change and our resistance to it! It's an intriguing question, and the answer lies in various psychological and biological factors.

As humans, we thrive on familiarity and predictability because our brains are wired to seek stability and reduce uncertainty. Change disrupts these patterns, triggering feelings of uncertainty and anxiety. Our evolutionary instincts kick in, prompting us to resist change as a self-protective mechanism.
Another reason for our resistance is that change often necessitates letting go of comfortable routines, habits, and beliefs. We develop a sense of identity and security around these familiar aspects of our lives. When faced with change, we fear losing that familiar sense of self or security, which can create resistance. Moreover, change often requires effort, adaptation, and learning new skills. Our brains are wired to conserve energy, so we naturally lean towards the path of least resistance. Change inherently requires

stepping out of our comfort zones, which can be uncomfortable and challenging.

Additionally, our past experiences can influence our attitude towards change. Negative experiences of change, such as failures or traumas, can lead to a fear of repeating those experiences, causing resistance. On the other hand, positive experiences with change can foster an openness and readiness to embrace it.

Lastly, organizational and societal factors can contribute to resistance to change. Fear of the unknown, lack of trust in leadership, unclear communication, and a perceived lack of control or involvement in the change process can all fuel resistance. Understanding our instinctual resistance to change is the first step towards managing it. By actively acknowledging and exploring the underlying reasons for our resistance, we can better navigate and embrace change. Practicing self-awareness, cultivating a growth mindset, and developing resilience can help us become more adaptable and open to change. So, while our nature may initially resist change vigorously, understanding the factors at play can enable us to overcome that resistance and embrace the opportunities and growth that change can bring.

Change is inevitable. It is an integral part of life that continuously shapes and molds our journeys. Yet, so often, we find ourselves fearing, and even avoiding change. We cling to what is known and familiar, hesitant to venture into the unknown. However, there is great power and liberation in embracing change with a shift in mindset.

Change is not something to be feared or avoided. It is an opportunity for growth, learning, and self-discovery. Just as the seasons change, bringing forth new beginnings and transformations, change in our lives opens doors to endless possibilities. It allows us to shed old skin, break free from stagnation, and evolve into better versions of ourselves.

To overcome the fear of change, it is crucial to recognize and acknowledge it. Reflect on the specific aspects of change that trigger anxiety within you. Is it the fear of the unknown? The fear of failure? The fear of leaving your comfort zone? Identifying the core elements of your fear will empower you to confront them head-on.

Cultivate Self-Awareness

Developing self-awareness is a powerful tool in overcoming the fear of change. Take the time to understand your strengths, weaknesses, and values. This introspection will help you gain clarity on what you truly want in life. Knowing yourself on a deep level will build confidence and resilience in the face of change.

Perhaps the greatest fear associated with change is the fear of failure. The only way to avoid that is not to do anything, not take any action and live as a spectator rather than as a protagonist. Making mistakes is part of the learning curve.

When we make mistakes we learn from these, making corrections and improving ourselves. When we learned to walk, we made thousands of attempts and failed a similar number of times. But this didn't stop us from trying again falling and learning how to get up again. No-one judged us when we weren't able to walk neither us nor others. Why not keep the same acceptance when faced with times we "fall" in life? It is the judgment and fear of that that paralyses us and falsifies our interpretation of events stopping us from moving forward. When we free ourselves from the emotional baggage transformation is made possible. Remember that the people who manage to achieve their dreams against all odds of success are those who worry less about failure. It is the people convinced that however things might go they will have learned something new along the way. In this way they enjoy the journey as much as getting to the destination itself.

How To Shift Your Mindset

Shifting your mindset can be essential in embracing change and reaching your full potential. Maintaining the same patterns can lead to feeling stuck in a specific part of your life. While it may feel comfortable to "be stuck", these situations often restrict our ability to grow. A growth mindset can be valuable when adapting to new situations because it promotes seeing challenges as opportunities for growth. This mindset often involves believing abilities and intelligence can be developed through work, dedication, and a willingness to learn. If you're needing a shift in your mindset, know that it might also involve embracing challenges as opportunities for growth rather than seeing them as threats.

Challenge Unwanted Thought Patterns

A common theme of fear-based mindsets is negativity. When adopting a growth mindset, try to challenge unwanted thoughts, identify negative self-talk, and replace them with more positive and empowering thoughts. For example, instead of thinking, "I can't do this," try thinking, "I may not be able to do this yet, but with practice and effort, I can learn and improve." This practice is called cognitive restructuring, a common strategy in cognitive-behavioral therapy (CBT).

Practice Positive Affirmations

Positive affirmations may also help you shift your mindset towards growth and positivity. Forbes quotes CJ Bathgate, Ph.D., a clinical psychologist in the Division of Neurology and Behavioral Health at National Jewish Health. He states, "A positive affirmation is a concise, realistic statement that embodies something we value, whether it's who we want to be or what we want in life. Our brains are always looking for shortcuts and tend to latch onto thoughts that come up the most or are the most easily available."

For example, repeating, "I am capable and resilient" or "I embrace change and growth" can help shift a mindset towards a more positive and growth-oriented point or perspective. By regularly practicing positive affirmations, individuals can build their self-confidence and resilience. This can help them overcome obstacles and imagine better ways to adapt to change.

Below are a few positive affirmations you can try for embracing change:

- "I commit to always trying my best."
- "I ma proud of myself."
- "I choose change, even when it's hard."
- "I will get through this change."
- "I am strong, capable, and worthy of positive change."
- "Change is a teacher."
- "I am on a journey and can't wait to see where I end up."

Focus On The Present Moment

In addition to challenging negative thoughts and practicing positive affirmations, try to focus on the present moment and cultivate gratitude for what you have. Mindfulness practices, such as meditation or deep breathing exercises, can help individuals stay present and reduce anxiety and stress. Additionally, taking enough time to reflect on what you're grateful for, such as your relationships, accomplishments, or personal strengths, can help you develop a more growth-oriented mindset.

Growth Mindset Vs Fixed Mindset

Having a growth mindset has become increasingly important. While a fixed mindset holds us back, a growth mindset is the key to unlocking our full potential. Let's explore the significance of cultivating a growth mindset and how it can positively impact various aspects of our lives.

Understanding the Mindset

To grasp the importance of a growth mindset, it's essential to differentiate it from a fixed mindset. A fixed mindset is characterized by the belief that abilities, intelligence, and talents are fixed traits that cannot be developed. On the other hand, a growth mindset is the belief that these qualities can be cultivated and developed over time through effort, perseverance, and learning.

A growth mindset empowers us to embrace challenges rather than shy away from them. Instead of viewing setbacks as failures, someone with a growth mindset sees them as opportunities for growth and learning. This mindset encourages us to persist in the face of difficulties and approach challenges with a sense of curiosity and determination. By embracing a growth mindset, we tap into our untapped potential. When we believe that our abilities can be developed, we are more likely to take on new experiences, push our boundaries, and strive for excellence. This mindset fosters a sense of resilience and enables us to harness our innate abilities to achieve success in various areas of life.

When we believe that intelligence and skills can be enhanced through effort and dedication, we approach every opportunity as a chance to expand our knowledge and expertise. This mindset drives us to seek out new information, engage in continuous self-improvement, and stay adaptable in a rapidly changing world. A growth mindset helps build resilience and a positive perspective. When faced with failure or setbacks, rather than becoming discouraged or giving up, individuals with a growth mindset view these experiences as valuable lessons. They understand that setbacks are temporary and that effort and perseverance can lead to progress and eventual success. This optimistic outlook allows for greater emotional well-being and a more positive approach to life's challenges. When we believe that people can grow and develop, we approach others with empathy, understanding, and a desire to help them succeed. This mindset fosters collaboration, constructive feedback, and a supportive environment that nurtures personal and collective growth.

The importance of a growth mindset cannot be overstated. By embracing the belief that our abilities can be developed through effort and learning, we unlock our potential, overcome challenges, achieve success, and foster resilience.

CHAPTER 2. DECLUTTERING YOUR ENVIRONMENT FOR MENTAL CLARITY

Have you ever noticed how much clearer and focused your mind is when it is not cluttered? A cluttered mind is restless and unfocused. It can mean your vision is clouded, as your mind is moving in different directions at once, adding to your stress level when very little gets done.

What about that jumble of excess stuff around you? Research has shown that physical clutter affects our brain's ability to concentrate and process information. Neuroscientists at Princeton University found that physical clutter in your surroundings competes for your attention, resulting in decreased performance and increased stress.

A study by UCLA's Center on Everyday Lives and Families (CELF) explored the relationship between 32 families and the thousands of objects in their homes and concluded that clutter has a strong effect on mood and self-esteem. The study found that the amount of stress the families experienced at home was directly proportional to the amount of stuff they possessed.

In the end, decluttering is the first step to creating more open space both physically and in your mind, enabling your mind to sharpen, focus better and lead to you taking better care of other aspects of life.

Life Declutter

Decluttering our spaces helps us feel calmer and allows more space for the relationships and experiences that bring us true joy and purpose. Having a clutter-free home and workspace can also help us be more productive and creative throughout the day, leading to better results in whatever we are pursuing, this sounds great, but what if you successfully declutter your environments but you still have a *cluttered mind*? Then how do we Declutter Your Mind & Keep It That Way?

Clutter in our minds is probably the worst kind of clutter because it fills up our brain and crowds out the capacity for simple tasks like remembering to take a lunch bag with us in the morning, let alone for more demanding tasks like writing or project managing. It happens because of mental fatigue, which is over-activity. The endless activity could be positive things like learning something new or diving into a project at work, or it might be negative things like worrying or over-analyzing or playing images of the past on repeat mode. Whether good or bad, the overdrive eventually catches up and depletes our mental energy and every inch of space in our brain.
As aggravating as a cluttered mind is, the worst part is that left unchecked, mental fatigue and brain clutter will lead to chronic stress and depression, which in turn can lead to chronic disease. It can also affect your relationships with others, both because you'll be less sociable and pleasant

and because your depleted energy will be draining on them as well, so make it a habit to develop a specific brain decluttering practice. It needn't be complex - even a few of these simple actions will reap positive benefits.

Decluttering your mind starts with a brain dump. It can last as quick as ten minutes. According to Tech Target,

"A brain dump is a complete transfer of accessible knowledge about a particular subject from your brain to some other storage medium, such as paper or your computer's hard drive."

Brain dumps is the best way to take everything going on in your head out onto paper. This can get yourself out of a state of overwhelm and confusion, and turn your mental paralysis into action.
By doing an effective brain dump, you release all of the information your brain tries to store and allows you to decide what is important. You only need to do brain dump for 10 minutes every day.
Each night when you are done for the day, do a brain dump exercise.
Use this information to build out your to do list for the next day. This also frees up your mind to focus on family and even sleep.You may find that when you get started with a brain dump, you have a hard time writing down what is in your mind.

At other times you may mass distribute the words in your head onto paper at rapid speed.

Whichever the case, grab a pen and paper and set the timer for ten minutes.

Whatever comes to your mind, write it down. Do not edit as you write or worry about grammar. By simply writing, you transfer all of that information and later you will read this information and store it as needed.

Write for ten minutes straight, if you cannot think of anything to write, write "I have nothing to write". Doing this keeps your pen to paper and opens up the creative flow.

Categorize your brain dump

Jotting everything down on paper and putting items into your calendar is the goal. It starts with looking at your brain-dump and identifying the themes.

- Are there projects / tasks on the paper?
- Which items are new ideas?
- Which items are work related, family related, or hobby related?

Create different categories and begin organizing each of the items on your brain-dump. Include a miscellaneous section for the random thoughts that you have.

When you start to organize your brain dump, you can see where your mind is focused and possibly where you need to spend more time.

An effective brain dump will allow you to focus on what matters. What you write down may not be relevant right now but you may need it at a future date.

Turn ideas into a to-do list

When you do your brain dumps at night, you are able to create your to-do list for the next day and set yourself up for success. Instead of showing up to work the next morning to get organized, you are ready to go and can jump right in.
While building your to-do list, you can either defer tasks to a later date or delegate them out.
Take a look at your calendar and start carving in the time. Identify the tasks that need to be done the next day or a few days later, focusing in on two to three major tasks a day. You can prioritize the tasks based on their importance and urgency.
When brain-dumping becomes a part of your life, you will notice that you're less overwhelmed and have more time to focus on tasks at hand. You will see a boost in your productivity and the quality of work. The less clutter, the sharper your brain, brain dumping is a great way to declutter your brain, from negative emotions to the tasks you work on each day.
At the end of your day, conduct a brain dump for ten minutes. Give yourself enough time after the brain dump to take a look at the tasks on your list.

Identify the tasks that have a high priority and cannot be delegated or deferred, and begin to place the high priority tasks into your calendar.
By focusing on the tasks each day, you know what you are working on and what your next step is. You will save a lot of time and energy by spending it on what matters.

One thing I found really helpful with mental clarity, was self talk. Talk to yourself like you would talk to your best friend. Isn't it strange how people can be nicer to their friends than they are to themselves? In some cases, if we spoke to our friends the way we speak to ourselves, we wouldn't have any friends.
Change the script by focusing on self-love and self-acceptance instead of self-judgment.

For instance:
- Instead of, "I bet my friends noticed how bid I've got," try, "I love my body no matter what size it is."
- Instead of, "There's no way they'd hire me," try, "I'd be a great candidate for that position."

Also keep an eye on your stress levels, thoughts and stress go hand-in-hand.
It's difficult to think positively when you're under high stress. And it's also difficult to manage your stress when you have too many negative thoughts.
That's why it's essential to prevent high stress before it starts in your mind. When you catch yourself thinking

about something stressful, immediately shift the focus to how resilient you are.

For instance:

- Instead of, "This project is too hard," try, "I can do anything I set my mind to."
- Instead of, "The clock is ticking, and I'll never finish this on time," try, "I've been on deadline before this is no big deal."

Today with what ever is going on in my life I always look on the bright side. Most experiences have a negative and a positive side if we look closely. You may not enjoy doing the washing, but you love having clean clothes to wear afterward. You may hate getting on planes, but you love exploring a new place once you land.

When you start focusing on the negative side of things, flip your thinking to the positive side.

For instance

- instead of, "That movie was bad," try, "That was a unique storyline."
- Instead of, "That sounds boring," try, "I'm looking forward to doing something different."

I believe that challenging your thoughts is the best way to see if they are true and logical. A great question to ask when you're experiencing this is: is there evidence to back up what I'm thinking?

If there's no logic to support those thoughts, change your point of view.

For instance:
* instead of, "They don't want me to go to the party," try, "They knew I planned on going out of town that weekend."
* Instead of, "I'm stuck, and I don't know what to do," try, "With a little creativity, I'll find a solution."

Why I Include positive self-talk as part of my morning routine is the benefits it can have for your overall well-being. Here are a few reasons why it can be beneficial:

* Boosts Confidence: Starting your day with positive self-talk can help build your self-confidence and self-esteem. By acknowledging your strengths and abilities, you set a positive tone for the day ahead.
* Sets a Positive Mindset: Positive self-talk can help you adopt a more positive mindset and approach challenges with optimism. It can shift your focus from negative thoughts or self-doubt to more constructive and empowering thoughts.

* Increases Motivation: When you believe in yourself and your abilities, you are more likely to feel motivated and inspired to pursue your goals. Positive self-talk can

provide the encouragement you need to take action and strive for success.
- Reduces Stress: Positive self-talk can counteract negative or critical thoughts that contribute to stress and anxiety. By replacing negative self-talk with positive affirmations, you can reduce stress levels and promote a calmer state of mind.
- Improves Overall Well-being: Regularly practicing positive self-talk can have a positive impact on your overall well-being. It can improve your mood, enhance your relationships with others, and increase your overall sense of happiness and fulfillment.

By incorporating positive self-talk into your morning routine, you are setting the stage for a more positive and productive day ahead.
Today I make it a priority to Weave it into my routine, make positive self talk part of your everyday routine.

CHAPTER 3: SETTING CLEAR AND ACHIEVABLE GOALS

Setting clear and achievable goals is a crucial step in achieving success in various aspects of our lives. Whether it's personal development, career growth, or even health and wellness, having well-defined goals helps provide direction and motivation.

Why should we set goals in the first place?
That is a good question worth answering, since nothing should be done in life if there isn't a real reason to do so. The value of goals lies in the direction and purpose they provide. When we set a goal, we are giving ourselves a target to strive for. Holding onto that end result leads to a more structured and purposeful life.
Many good qualities stem from goal setting. Once a goal is set, motivation is needed to work towards it every day.

Focus also must be put into practice

By giving ourselves goals to work towards, days become more meaningful and productive. Without a clear goal, it is difficult to generate a plan. And without a plan, it is likely we will not be as efficient.

Anything can be a Goal!

This is one of the most beautiful aspects of goal setting. While many believe that in order to set a goal it must be large, that is simply not the case. We can apply goal setting to any part of our lives.

By having goals in place, we drastically improve our chances of success. Since structure, focus, and direction are all a result of setting goals. From large scale goals to smaller daily ones, the value is the same. Having a clear-cut plan for life increases the likelihood of us achieving what we want. It can also lead to a more fulfilling life.

In my experience, I have found that setting goals makes me feel happier and more productive. My large goals lead to daily tasks I wish to accomplish. At the end of the day, there is nothing better than looking over my list and seeing all I accomplished that day.

So, there is no shortage of value found in goal setting and the benefits gained from it are equally as impressive.

Benefits of Goal Setting

We now know what goal setting is and the value it provides. But what about the benefits gained from the practice? After setting goals, there are many benefits that can be expected. They include the following:

Increases Motivation

Goals work to increase our motivation in two ways. First, they give us a target to work towards. Having an objective instills a certain level of motivation in us to achieve it.

Second, with each goal that we accomplish, whether large or small, our motivation grows. This is due to the sense of pride felt in achieving a target, which then motivates us to do it more and more.

Provides a Sense of Responsibility

Taking personal responsibility for our lives is very important to our success and overall well-being. When we set goals, we are giving ourselves something to work for. The goal is our own making, which means accomplishing it will be by our own result.
In order to achieve our goals, we know what must be done. The daily tasks involved are important, and we are the only ones who are responsible as to whether or not they get done. Having this responsibility in life is truly powerful and freeing.

"Taking personal responsibility for our lives is very important to our success and overall well-being. When we set goals, we are giving ourselves something to work for. The goal is our own making, which means accomplishing it will be by our own result."

Allows You to Track Progress

This one is especially true for smaller goals. In my experience, a lot of times what can happen when I just set a large target is that I will get frustrated along the way and wind up quitting. The reason this happens is due to the inability to see all the little progress made along the way. By setting small goals, we can keep track of all the work we've done. Even if it is a matter of progressing inch by inch, this will help keep us motivated and on track towards the larger goal.

Forces You to Set Priorities

In life, priorities are key if we want to accomplish anything. You must set priorities for yourself as to not get distracted. Setting goals really helps do just that.

When we set a large goal, and then subsequent smaller ones, there are certain priorities that become apparent. For example, to achieve a goal of losing weight or building muscle, exercise must become a priority.

Likewise, if there is a goal to increase our income then making more money has to become a priority. The process of setting goals immediately outlines what will become a priority in our lives.

With the value placed on goal setting and the addition of these four benefits, it is easy to see its importance. The question now is, how should we go about goal setting? Seems like a pretty simple construct, though a set of guidelines is always useful.

That is why we want our goals to be SMART: specific, measurable, achievable, relevant, and time bound.

To ensure that your goals are clear and achievable, follow the SMART goal-setting framework.

WHAT'S YOUR GOAL? Remember to be S.M.A.R.T.!
Specific - What exactly are you going to do?
Measurable - You need to be able to track progress; this can be framed by 'how much or how many'.
Achievable - Be realistic; losing 10 lbs. in 3 months is achievable, where losing 10 lbs. in 3 days is not achievable.
Relevant - Your goal should be important to you.
Time-based - When do you want to accomplish your goal? Select a date in the future.

Here are four steps to follow to get you started.

Identifying Your Objectives

The first step to setting clear and achievable goals is identifying and defining your objectives. Start by asking yourself what you want to achieve or change in a specific area of your life. It could be related to your career, personal relationships, health, or any other area that requires improvement. Be specific and realistic about what you want to accomplish.

Breaking Down Goals Into Actionable Steps

Once you have defined your goals, break them down into smaller, actionable steps. This process makes the goals less overwhelming and helps you create a clear path towards achieving them. Start by identifying the tasks or milestones that need to be completed to reach each goal. Assign deadlines to each step and prioritize them according to their importance.

Visualize and Track Progress

Visualizing your goals helps create a sense of ownership and commitment. Use tools like vision boards or written descriptions to remind yourself of your objectives and the outcomes you desire. Additionally, track your progress regularly. Celebrate small achievements along the way and learn from any setbacks or challenges you may encounter.

Flexibility and Adaptation

Keep in mind that goals are not set in stone. Be open to adjusting or modifying them as circumstances change or new insights arise. It's essential to strike a balance between being flexible and staying committed to your objectives. Embrace the journey and be willing to make necessary adjustments to set yourself up for success.

CHAPTER 4. DESIGNING YOUR IDEAL MORNING ROUTINE

How you start each morning has a huge impact – positively or negatively on the rest of your day. By practicing a healthy morning routine, you can increase your productivity, decrease stress, boost happiness and more. Too many people wake up each day to a barrage of responsibilities that end up dictating the flow of their mornings. If you have kids or pets, you need to care for them. Most people have morning chores, need to make breakfast, get ready for work, and so on. I am not suggesting you shirk your responsibilities. But the truth is, you will be better prepared to handle everything on your plate each morning, if you start with a healthy self-care routine.

The first step to kicking your day off right is adjusting your sleep schedule to ensure you have enough time in the morning for yourself and your responsibilities. If your kids get up at 6:30 a.m., this means getting up before them. Or, even if you don't have kids or pets to care for, if you usually get up at 7 a.m. to scramble out the door by 7:30, it's time for you to start your days earlier.

That said, sleep is important. When you adjust your alarm to wake up sooner, you also need to adjust your bedtime to turn in earlier. There is nothing healthy about being sleep deprived, so aim to get at least seven hours of sleep.

Let's look a bit more about the importance of getting the right amount of sleep.

Sleep is a fundamental aspect of our overall health and well-being. Getting an adequate amount of quality sleep plays a vital role in maintaining physical health, supporting cognitive function, and promoting emotional balance. In this chapter, we will explore the importance of having the correct sleep schedule, the benefits it brings, and some practical tips to establish healthy sleep habits.

✳ Regulating Circadian Rhythm:
Our bodies have an internal biological clock called the circadian rhythm, which regulates our sleep-wake cycle. Maintaining a consistent sleep schedule helps align this rhythm, making it easier to fall asleep and wake up naturally. By going to bed and waking up at the same time each day, our bodies establish a routine and optimize the quality of sleep.

✳ Enhancing Sleep Quality:
Having the correct sleep schedule contributes to overall sleep quality. Consistency in sleep patterns allows our body to get the amount of rest it needs, resulting in improved energy levels, focus, and concentration. Additionally, a regular sleep schedule promotes better sleep architecture, including the proper balance between deep sleep and REM sleep, which are essential for physical and mental restoration.

❋ Improving Performance and Productivity:
A well-regulated sleep schedule positively impacts our daytime performance and productivity. A good night's sleep improves cognitive functions such as memory, attention, learning, and problem-solving abilities. By being well-rested, we experience enhanced creativity, decision-making skills, and overall mental agility, leading to increased performance in various areas of life.

❋ Supporting Physical Health:
Having the correct sleep schedule is closely linked to maintaining physical health. Adequate sleep provides our bodies with the time necessary for repairing and rejuvenating tissues, regulating hormone levels, and supporting immune system functions. Chronic sleep deprivation has been associated with numerous health issues, including obesity, diabetes, cardiovascular diseases, and weakened immune function.

❋ Promoting Emotional Well-being:
Sleep also greatly influences our emotional well-being. A consistent sleep schedule helps stabilize mood and contributes to better emotional regulation. Lack of quality sleep often leads to irritability, mood swings, increased stress levels, and a higher likelihood of experiencing anxiety or depression. Prioritizing a healthy sleep routine ensures we can approach each day with a positive mindset and emotional resilience.

✺ Tips for Establishing Healthy Sleep Habits:
To establish the correct sleep schedule, consider the following tips:

- ✺ Set a consistent bedtime and wake-up time, even on weekends.
- ✺ Create a soothing pre-sleep routine to signal your body that it's time to unwind. This can include activities such as reading, taking a warm bath, or practicing relaxation exercises.
- ✺ Make sure your sleeping environment is comfortable, quiet, cool, and dark.
- ✺ Avoid consuming stimulants such as caffeine or nicotine close to bedtime.
- ✺ Limit the use of electronic devices, as the blue light emitted can disrupt sleep patterns.
- ✺ Engage in regular physical exercise, but avoid vigorous activity close to bedtime.
- ✺ Avoid heavy meals and excessive fluid intake close to bedtime to prevent discomfort or nighttime awakenings.

Before you can start creating your "perfect" morning routine you need to review your current one.
Believe it or not, you already have a morning routine. If you pay attention, you'll notice you do almost the same exact thing every morning.
Hitting snooze every morning may be part of your routine. Not eating breakfast or running out the door could also be a part of your routine.

Let's take some time to examine your current routine.

Ask yourself these questions:

- How early do you get up?
- Do you have enough time to get ready before work/school?
- Are you getting enough sleep?
- Do you feel refreshed and ready to tackle the day?
- Do you eat breakfast every morning?

If you want to stick to a new routine, you need to define your why. Why do you want to create a morning routine? When you're struggling to get out of bed, remembering why it's important to you will be super helpful.
Maybe it's because you don't want to feel rushed out the door every morning. Or you want more time with your kids before they run to catch the bus. Or you want to start your day with some personal development time.
Whatever it is, write it down.

In my first book "Morning Game Changer" I designed a morning routine called "W.I.N.N.E.R".

Here's an expanded version of each element:

W - Water/Hydrate: Start your day by hydrating your body. Drink a glass of water upon waking up to replenish and rehydrate your system.

I - Immediate Wins: Begin your morning by accomplishing small tasks or goals that can give you an immediate sense of accomplishment. This could be something as simple as making your bed, organizing your workspace, or completing a short exercise routine.

N - Nurture Your Goals: Take some time in the morning to review your goals and set intentions for the day. Visualize what you want to achieve and align your actions accordingly.

N - Nutritious Breakfast: Fuel your body with a nutritious and well-balanced breakfast to provide the energy needed for the day ahead. Include foods rich in protein, whole grains, fruits, and vegetables to support mental and physical well-being.

E - Exercise: Incorporate physical activity into your morning routine. This could involve a workout session, a brisk walk, yoga, or any form of exercise that suits your preference. Engaging in exercise can boost your energy, mood, and overall productivity.

R - Reflection: Dedicate a few minutes for reflection and introspection. This can involve practicing mindfulness, journaling, or meditating. Reflect on your thoughts, feelings, and experiences. This helps promote self-awareness, calmness, and mental clarity.

Feel free to adjust or adapt this routine to fit your personal needs and preferences. Remember, the key is to establish habits that support a positive start to your day and set you up for success.

Here's a few tips to help you get started.

To start building your own morning routine, you can consider a few key factors:

- Identify your goals: What do you want to achieve with your morning routine? Do you want to improve productivity, focus on self-care, or enhance physical well-being? Recognizing your goals will help determine the activities and habits to include in your routine.

- Consider your preferences: Think about activities that energize and motivate you. Do you prefer a workout, mindfulness practices, reading, or any other activity? Choose actions that resonate with your interests and passions.

- Prioritize self-care: Dedicate time in your routine for activities that prioritize your well-being. This can include hydrating, stretching, meditating, or simply enjoying a calm and quiet moment to start your day on a positive note.

✳ Gradual implementation: Start by incorporating a few activities into your morning routine and gradually add more over time. This allows for a realistic and sustainable integration of new habits.

Remember, everyone's morning routine will be unique. Experiment with different activities, durations, and orders to find what works best for you. With consistency and commitment, your personalized morning routine can become a powerful tool to kickstart your day and set a positive tone for the rest of your day. Happy building!

CHAPTER 5. THE POWER OF PRIORITIZATION: FOCUS ON WHAT MATTERS

It is so easy to become overwhelmed with the sheer number of tasks and responsibilities vying for our attention every day. Amidst this chaos, the power of prioritization emerges as a guiding force, allowing us to focus on what truly matters. By consciously giving importance to our tasks and organizing our time, we can unlock the key to success and lead a balanced and fulfilling life.

The Impact of Prioritization

Prioritization is not just about organizing tasks in order of importance. It is a mindset that enables us to allocate our limited resources, such as time and energy, in the most effective and efficient way. When we prioritize, we are able to identify our goals and align our actions accordingly. This clarity helps to reduce stress, increase productivity, and achieve better outcomes in both personal and professional domains.

Identifying What Truly Matters

To harness the power of prioritization, it is vital to identify what truly matters to us. This involves defining our long-term goals and values and understanding how each task or responsibility aligns with them. By focusing on activities that align with our core values, we can create a sense of purpose and fulfillment in our lives. It is also crucial to differentiate between urgent tasks and important tasks. Urgent tasks may demand immediate attention, but important tasks contribute more significantly to our long-term goals.

Strategies for Effective Prioritization

- Evaluate and Assess: Take a step back and evaluate the tasks and responsibilities at hand. Consider the desired outcomes, timelines, and resources required for each task. Assess their relevance and potential impact on your long-term goals.

- Set Clear Priorities: Once you have evaluated your tasks, set clear priorities. Assign each task a level of importance based on its alignment with your goals and values. This will help you determine where to invest your time and energy.

- Pareto Principle: Apply the 80/20 rule, also known as the Pareto Principle, which states that 80% of your results come from 20% of your efforts. Identify the tasks that fall within this 20% and prioritize them accordingly.

- Delegate and Eliminate: Recognize tasks that can be delegated to others, freeing up your time for more important matters. Additionally, identify tasks that are less relevant and can be eliminated altogether, providing even more room for meaningful actions.

- Focus on Quality, not Quantity: It is better to tackle a few high-priority tasks with full attention and commitment rather than overwhelming ourselves with a long list of tasks that may not contribute significantly to our goals.

- Time Blocking: Allocate specific time blocks for each task, ensuring uninterrupted focus and better productivity. This also helps in avoiding multitasking, which can decrease efficiency.

Once you're clear on your priorities, you've got to protect your time by sayings no to distractions. This is an ongoing process because distractions are everywhere! From the moment we wake up, we're bombarded with notifications and requests and people shouting for our attention. In our world of instant connection and overstimulation, it's possible to be distracted every single moment of the day. Staying focused in a frantic world is a choice. Don't reprioritize what's most important to you based on the last-minute requests from other people. Don't let good opportunities derail you from the best opportunities. Don't say yes when you really want to say no.

By the way, it's important to recognize that we say yes to distractions for all sorts of reasons. Maybe we don't want to

disappoint anyone, or we feel pressure to achieve, or we want to be the hero. Or maybe it's a combination of unhealthy motivations and a true desire to grow and experience life. What about you? Why do you say yes? And what keeps you from saying no?
Always remember: when you say no to something, it frees you up to say yes to what matters most.

Prioritization is not just about organizing your tasks and responsibilities; it is a powerful tool that can significantly impact your mindset and life. When you make a conscious effort to prioritize, you take control of your time, focus on what truly matters, and create a foundation for success.

Here's how prioritizing helped change my mindset and life

It helped me gain clarity on what is most important to me, and helped me define my goals, align my actions accordingly. Instead of feeling overwhelmed by a never-ending to-do list, prioritization allowed me to focus on the tasks that truly matter. This clarity and focus created a sense of purpose, making me more determined and motivated. I prioritized tasks based on their importance and urgency, I then become more efficient and productive. By concentrating on the vital few tasks that contribute the most to my goals, I avoided wasting time on trivial matters. This boost in productivity leads to a sense of achievement and fulfillment as I accomplished meaningful work.

I found that one of the most significant benefits of prioritization is the reduction of stress and overwhelm. When I have a clear list of tasks in order of importance, it becomes easier to manage my workload, I can tackle each task methodically, without the constant worry of missing something crucial. The feeling of control over my time and responsibilities provided me with a sense of calmness and confidence. The longer I practiced prioritizing, I developed a better ability to assess and make informed decisions. I become skilled at distinguishing between tasks that are important and those that can be put aside. This skill of effective decision-making can extend beyond task management and positively influence other aspects of your life.

Also by identifying your priorities, I can allocate time and energy to the essential aspects of my life, such as relationships, personal development, and self-care. Balancing my personal and professional responsibilities leads to increased satisfaction and overall well-being.

By focusing on my most important tasks, I made consistent progress towards my objectives. This practice builds momentum and a positive mindset, reinforcing the belief that you have the ability to achieve what you set out to do. Prioritization taught me to adapt to changing circumstances without losing sight of my goals, and now I regularly review and re-evaluate my priorities, and become more flexible in adjusting my plans. This mindset shift allowed me to adapt to unexpected challenges while keeping my focus on what truly matters in the long run.

Remember, prioritization is a personal process and requires consistent practice. It may take time to develop the habit, but the benefits are well worth the effort. By prioritizing your tasks and responsibilities, you can transform your mindset, increase your productivity, reduce stress, and create a more fulfilling and successful life.

CHAPTER 6. DEVELOPING EFFECTIVE TIME MANAGEMENT STRATEGIES

Do you often feel stressed out with too much work to do when there's not enough time in the day? How is it then that some people seem to have enough time to do everything? The secret seems to be controlling time instead of letting time control you. In other words, the difference lies ineffective time management.

I understand that creating a successful morning routine requires more than just setting the alarm clock earlier. It necessitates a skillful approach to time management and the cultivation of organizational habits that will set the tone for a productive and fulfilling day.

Within this chapter, you will discover the power of effective time management techniques that will help you make the most of your mornings, I will delve into strategies for prioritizing tasks, setting attainable goals, and creating a schedule tailor-made for your unique needs and aspirations. By learning how to allocate and maximize your time, you will unlock a world of possibilities and achieve greater success in all areas of your life.
So what is Time Management and what are the benefits of this for me?
Time management is a technique for using your time productively and efficiently. It means organizing and

planning how to divide your time between various tasks. You'll have time to do everything you need without being stressed out about it with good time management skills. You can work productively and prioritize your time to work out the urgent or important tasks first while following up with things that are not urgent but still important. Thus, you can focus your time and energy on things that matter the most. You'll end up working smarter, not harder, to increase productivity.

Time management skills are essential because it helps us use time wisely and stop wasting time. We become more focused and productive when we are in charge of how we use our time. Productivity leads to profitability. So, good time management can add to your bottom line. The benefits of effective time management are immense:

- Less stress or anxiety
- Better work-life balance
- Increased focus
- Higher levels of productivity
- More free time
- Makes things simple and easy
- Less distraction
- Greater energy and motivation

Good time management begins with the right set of skills. You cannot manage your time better if you don't develop the essential time management skills. These skills take time to create and will vary from person to person. Finding what works best for your personality trait is necessary.

Let's analyze the core time management skills and how to develop them. I know some of this skills have already been mentioned in previous chapters, but it well worth going through them again.

Make a Plan

Effective time management isn't achieved randomly. It involves a good amount of planning. Developing a strategy for which tasks are important, task sequences, calendar management, meetings, project plans, etc., can help you calibrate the course of the day and not go astray.

Create a Priority List Rather Than a To-Do List

Think about what needs to be done and prioritize the most critical tasks. Refrain from creating to-do list of all tasks to be done. Instead, create a list of the tasks based on priority and check off items as you complete them. This helps to drive a sense of accomplishment and motivation. The best way to develop planning skills is using calendar tools like Google calendar.

Start Early

Start your day early to take full advantage of the day. Most successful people get up early in the morning and do some quick exercising before heading to work. If you start early, you have plenty of time to think and plan the day. Early in the morning, you are more calm, creative, and clear-headed. This means you have all the ingredients to be more productive.

Breakdown Every Task Into Small Chunks

Zero in on what you want, and build smaller goals that ladder up to your desired goal. Group all related tasks into smaller groups that are easy to manage and tackle. Thus, you can better visualize and take steps to reach your goal.

Practice Decision Making

What we do with the 24 hours in a day is what makes the real difference in time management. The ability for good decision-making about time is one of the top time management skills. Prioritize and decide which tasks to handle first and say no to.

Delegate tasks

Task delegation means proper management of tasks. Learning how to delegate is very important in developing time management skills. Delegating work to your subordinates depending on their skills and abilities will free up time for you and make your team members feel valued and motivated to perform well. By delegating or outsourcing whenever possible, you give yourself time to take on the most challenging tasks. Thus you move closer to the goal of becoming the most efficient version of yourself possible.

Set SMART Goals

Set goals that are specific, measurable, achievable, realistic, and secured within a time frame. Be specific with the outcomes you want to achieve and allocate the time needed to reach that outcome.

Set Up Deadlines

Set realistic deadlines for task completion and stick to them. Try to set a deadline before the due date to deal with other tasks that may get in the way.

Be Mindful of When You're Going Off-Track

Procrastination affects productivity and causes wastage of time and energy. We tend to procrastinate when bogged down or feeling bored. Break up challenging tasks into smaller activities to stay engaged and on track.

Learn to Set Boundaries and Say No

Time is your most precious asset, and good time management means getting comfortable with saying 'no' to tasks that are not your priority. Saying no on-time saves you time to focus on more important things. Learn how to set boundaries for yourself, so you don't end up biting more than you can chew.

Minimize Distractions

Anything that distracts you - emails, texts, social media - can make you lose focus and become less productive. Eliminate these distractions and take control of your time so you can get more work done.

Deal With Stress Wisely

Stress can affect our productivity. We often feel stressed when we take on more work than we can accomplish. It's crucial to identify what works for you when it comes to managing stress response. Find effective ways to deal with stress, including taking a short break, exercising, meditating, practicing a hobby, calling up a friend, or listening to music.

Avoid Multitasking

Multitasking sounds like you're getting more tasks at once. But, studies have proven that it actually hampers productivity. Therefore, rather than multitasking and splitting your attention between a few different tasks, focus on getting one task done and moving on to the next. This small change can improve your outcomes. Bonus: You'll feel less drained!

Use the 20-Minute Rule

The 20 minute increment block is one of the most essential time management skills. Prepare to tackle an important task and set the alarm for 20 minutes. Focus singularly on the task and give it your best shot until the alarm rings. Now decide if you're going to put the task down or finish it. Repeat until you've completed the task.

Take Time Off

Sometimes the best thing to do is give your mind a break from the task at hand. Taking a break is a great way to give your brain a chance to reset. It enhances focus and creativity and results in better problem-solving.

Build a System and Follow It Diligently

Try out different techniques and figure out what suits you the best. Put the selected methods together to build a system that works and helps you improve. Follow the system regularly to get the most value out of it.

Some of you will be already are using Time management skills you previously set up, but Remember, improving time management skills is an ongoing process that requires self-discipline and commitment. By implementing these strategies consistently, listed below you can achieve your goals more effectively and improve your time management skills:

Prepare and follow a schedule strictly

Create a daily or weekly schedule outlining your tasks and commitments. Understand the time needed for each task and assign specific time slots. Make a conscious effort to adhere to your schedule as closely as possible to maintain organization and focus.

Set boundaries for yourself

Learn to say no to tasks or activities that don't align with your priorities or goals. Set clear boundaries with others to avoid unnecessary interruptions or distractions. Protect your time by minimizing time-wasting activities such as excessive social media browsing or aimless web surfing.

Fix deadlines

Assign deadlines to your tasks, whether they are personal or work-related. Assigning deadlines helps create a sense of urgency and enables you to prioritize your work effectively. Be sure to set realistic deadlines considering each task's complexity and importance.

Set long- and short-term goals

Define your long-term goals clearly and break them into smaller, actionable short-term ones. Having specific goals provides clarity and motivation. Set deadlines for achieving your goals and regularly review your progress:

Manage your calendar effectively

Use a calendar or a digital planning tool to manage your appointments, deadlines, and important dates. Dedicate specific blocks of time for different activities, including work, breaks, and personal time. Regularly review and update your calendar to stay on top of your commitments.

Prioritize your assignments

Determine which tasks are most important and need immediate attention. Prioritizing helps you focus on high-value activities and prevents you from getting overwhelmed by less important tasks. Consider using techniques like the Eisenhower Matrix to categorize tasks based on urgency and importance.

Practice effective delegation

Learn to delegate tasks to others when appropriate. Identify and assign tasks that can be done by someone else. This will help you focus on higher-priority tasks and improves overall productivity.

Minimize multitasking

While it may seem efficient, multitasking often leads to decreased productivity and lower-quality work. Instead, focus on one task and then move on to the next. This approach helps maintain concentration and produces better results.

Take regular breaks

Avoid long stretches of continuous work as it can lead to burnout and decreased productivity. Take short breaks between tasks to recharge your mind and body. Use these breaks for relaxation, physical activity, or any activity that helps you rejuvenate.Learn from your experiences:

Engage in self-reflection to evaluate how you allocate your time and identify areas where you can make improvements.

Assess your productivity patterns and identify any recurring time-wasting activities or habits. Use this self-reflection to adjust your approach and continually refine your time management skills.

CHAPTER 7. OVERCOMING PROCRASTINATION: TAKING ACTION NOW

Ah, procrastination, the timeless foe of productivity. Overcoming this common challenge requires understanding its roots and implementing strategies to combat it. During procrastination, we tell ourselves all sorts of lies to justify our actions.

The first step to overcoming procrastination is to admit that you are avoiding the tasks that you are supposed to be doing. It's pretty common to procrastinate in all aspects of our lives, whether that means scrambling to finish a work project or putting off going to the gym or doing laundry. We know what we *want* to do, but something gets in the way. We get distracted or say "oh it's fine, I'll just do it later." It's no surprise the word procrastinate comes from the Latin word meaning "belonging to tomorrow."

The problem, however, is that procrastination isn't like other forms of distraction. An ill-timed call or meeting might interrupt your day. But true procrastination is an *emotional* problem that comes from within.

You can't put do-not-disturb mode on your boredom or anxiety, which means we're susceptible to procrastination anywhere and at any time. According to Timothy Pychyl, a professor who studies procrastination at Carleton University in Ottawa, procrastination has less to do with time management and more about our emotions.

We all try to avoid negative feelings in life–boredom, anxiety, or frustration. And we're more likely to put off work that makes us feel these ways.
So what do we do instead? We latch onto things that encourage positive feelings. We watch funny videos, lose ourselves in the adventure of video games, chat with friends, or do small busywork that gives us a hit of dopamine.
In short, procrastination makes you choose positive emotions now over putting in the hard work on truly meaningful work. Procrastination is a common phenomenon, but have you ever wondered why we tend to procrastinate, even when we know it's not in our best interests? While many of us may attribute it to external factors that hinder our progress, the true reasons behind procrastination go beyond mere obstacles. Let's explore some of the underlying causes that contribute to our tendency to put things off.

One reason for procrastination is the fear of failure or fear of not meeting expectations. We may worry about the outcome of a task and delay starting it as a means of avoiding the potential disappointment or judgment associated with it. By postponing the task, we temporarily protect ourselves from facing the fear head-on.

Another contributing factor to procrastination is the lack of motivation or interest in the task at hand. If we don't find a task engaging or meaningful, it becomes challenging to summon the necessary drive to begin or complete it. Without a sense of purpose or enthusiasm, we often find ourselves easily distracted and prone to postponing the task.

Moreover, our brain's inherent preference for short-term rewards can also lead to procrastination. We are naturally inclined towards immediate gratification, seeking activities that provide instant pleasure or relief. Tasks that require effort, concentration, or long-term commitment may pale in comparison to the allure of instant gratification, leading us to procrastinate.

Additionally, overwhelming tasks or a lack of proper planning and organization can contribute to procrastination. When faced with a daunting project or an unclear path forward, we may feel overwhelmed and uncertain of where to begin. This sense of being unprepared or unsure about the next steps can lead to avoidance and procrastination.

Understanding the reasons behind procrastination can help us address and overcome this tendency. By recognizing the fears, finding motivation, managing rewards, and improving our planning and organizational skills, we can gradually reduce procrastination and improve our productivity.

Overcoming procrastination can be challenging, but with some strategies and techniques, it is possible to develop better habits and improve productivity. Here are some effective ways to combat procrastination:

* Set Clear Goals: Clearly define your goals and break them down into manageable tasks. Setting specific, measurable, achievable, relevant, and time-bound (SMART) goals can help you stay focused and motivated.

* Prioritize and Create a Schedule: Determine which tasks are most important and prioritize them. Create a schedule or to-do list to allocate specific blocks of time for each task. Stick to the schedule as much as possible to avoid procrastination.

* Use Time Management Techniques: Explore time management techniques like the Pomodoro Technique, which involves working in focused 25-minute intervals with short breaks in between. This method can help you maintain concentration and make tasks more manageable.

* Overcome Perfectionism: Sometimes, the fear of not doing things perfectly can lead to procrastination. Recognize that perfection is not always attainable and focus on progress rather than perfection. Embrace the idea of "done is better than perfect."

- Break Tasks into Smaller Steps: Large tasks can be overwhelming and lead to procrastination. Break them down into smaller, more manageable steps. Completing these smaller steps provides a sense of progress and makes the task seem less daunting.

- Eliminate Distractions: Identify and minimize distractions that pull your focus away from the task at hand. Put away your phone, close unnecessary tabs on your computer, and create a designated, quiet workspace to help you concentrate.

- Find Accountability Partners: Share your goals and progress with someone you trust, such as a friend, family member, or colleague. Having an accountability partner can provide support and encouragement, and help keep you on track.

- Reward Yourself: Create a system of rewards for completing tasks or reaching milestones. Treat yourself to something enjoyable after completing a challenging task. Positive reinforcement can increase motivation and combat procrastination.

- Practice Self-Reflection: Take the time to reflect on your reasons for procrastination. Identify any underlying fears, beliefs, or patterns that contribute to your tendency to procrastinate. Developing self-awareness can help you address these issues and find effective solutions.

* Seek Support and Resources: If you find that procrastination is significantly impacting your life and productivity, consider seeking support from a therapist, counselor, or productivity coach. They can provide guidance, tools, and strategies tailored to your specific situation.

Remember, overcoming procrastination requires effort, consistency, and patience. By implementing these strategies and maintaining a proactive mindset, you can gradually improve your ability to manage tasks and stay focused.

If you don't want to do something, make a deal with yourself to do at least five minutes of it. After five minutes, you'll end up doing the whole thing.

CHAPTER 8. HARNESSING THE POWER OF HABITS FOR PRODUCTIVITY

If you haven't read "The Power of Habit by Charles Duhigg", I highly recommend you buy yourself a copy. This book is a captivating exploration of the science behind habits and their profound impact on our lives, both personally and professionally. Through engaging narratives and compelling research, Duhigg unveils the mechanisms that shape our habits and provides valuable insights into how we can transform our behaviors and achieve lasting change.

The book begins by delving into the nature of habits, explaining how they are formed and how they influence our daily routines. Duhigg introduces the habit loop, which consists of a cue, a routine, and a reward. He demonstrates how habits are deeply ingrained in our brains and how they can be modified by understanding and manipulating this loop.

Duhigg explores the power of keystone habits, which are pivotal habits that have a cascading effect on other areas of our lives. He presents examples of how changing a single keystone habit, such as exercise or mindfulness, can lead to positive transformations in various aspects, including productivity, health, and relationships.

The book also highlights the role of habits in organizational settings. Duhigg explains how successful companies and leaders utilize the power of habits to drive innovation, productivity, and positive work culture. He provides fascinating case studies, such as the transformation of Alcoa under the leadership of Paul O'Neill, to illustrate the impact of habits on organizational success.

Duhigg explores the neurology and psychology behind habit formation, offering insights into how our brains create and reinforce habits. He discusses the role of cravings and rewards in shaping habitual behaviors and provides strategies for replacing undesirable habits with healthier alternatives.

Furthermore, the book examines the concept of "small wins" and their role in habit change. Duhigg explains how focusing on small, achievable goals can lead to a sense of accomplishment and reinforce positive behaviors. He emphasizes the importance of tracking progress and celebrating milestones as a way to stay motivated and build momentum.

Let me explain a little about the "The Habit Loop": According to Duhigg, habits are formed through a three-step process known as the "habit loop".

Charles Duhigg introduces the concept of the Habit Loop, which is a three-step process that explains how habits are formed and why they are so powerful. The three steps in the Habit Loop are cue, routine, and reward.

Cue

The cue is the trigger that signals our brain to go into automatic mode and initiate a specific habit. It can be any external or internal stimulus that prompts us to engage in a particular behavior. Cues can take various forms, such as a specific time of day, a particular location, an emotional state, or even the presence of certain people.

Routine

The routine represents the actual behavior or action that is performed in response to the cue. This is the habitual pattern that we engage in, often without much conscious thought or effort. The routine can range from simple actions like scrolling through social media, to more complex behaviors like exercising or meditating.

Reward

The reward is the positive reinforcement that follows the routine. It is the reason why the habit loop becomes ingrained in our brains. Rewards are typically associated with pleasurable sensations, feelings of accomplishment, or some form of gratification. The reward helps to solidify the habit in our minds and motivates us to repeat the behavior in the future.

The Habit Loop and Habit Formation

According to Duhigg, understanding the Habit Loop is essential in understanding how habits are formed and how they can be changed or manipulated. By analyzing and unpacking each element of the loop, we can identify the cues, routines, and rewards that drive our habits.

Duhigg suggests that to change or replace a habit, we need to keep the same cue and reward but modify the routine in between. By experimenting with different routines while maintaining the same cue and reward, we can gradually replace unwanted habits with more desirable ones.

For example, if the cue is stress (cue), the routine is indulging in unhealthy snacks (routine), and the reward is feeling momentarily relieved (reward), we can experiment with replacing the routine of unhealthy snacking with a healthier alternative like going for a short walk or practicing deep breathing.

By recognizing the cues that trigger our routines and the rewards that reinforce them, we can gain insight into our habits and have the ability to reshape them to align with our goals and aspirations.
Let's explore some key psychological factors that significantly influence productivity:

- Habits hold incredible power over our actions. Leveraging productive habits allows us to automate routine tasks, freeing up valuable mental energy for more critical endeavors. By consciously cultivating positive habits, we can streamline our workflow and propel productivity to new heights.

- Motivation: Motivation serves as the backbone of productivity. Understanding what truly inspires and drives us is key to unlocking our full potential. By pinpointing our motivators and employing effective strategies to boost motivation, we can overcome obstacles and realize our aspirations, elevating our productivity along the way.

- Emotions: Emotions wield a significant impact on our productivity. Learning to manage our emotions effectively empowers us to navigate challenges, reduce stress, and cultivate an environment conducive to focus and motivation. By fostering emotional intelligence, we can channel our emotions towards productive outcomes, optimizing our performance.

- Mindset: Our mindset serves as the compass that guides our productivity journey. A growth mindset fuels resilience, embraces challenges as opportunities for growth, and propels us towards success. Conversely, a fixed mindset limits progress. By cultivating a growth mindset, we unlock our capacity to overcome obstacles, embrace continuous improvement, and achieve remarkable productivity breakthroughs.

By comprehending and harnessing these psychological factors, we gain valuable insights that can revolutionize our productivity strategies. With this knowledge, we can develop personalized approaches tailored to our unique needs, optimizing our workflow and propelling us towards our goals.

Let's move on to productivity.

Productivity is the foundation of success and accomplishment. It is the art of effectively managing our time, energy, and resources to achieve our goals. However, productivity is not merely a result of motivation or willpower; rather, it is heavily influenced by the habits we cultivate. In this chapter, we will explore the significance of habits in promoting productivity and discuss practical strategies to harness their power for optimal success.

Understanding the Power of Habits

Habits are deeply ingrained behavioral patterns that we develop over time through repetition. They act as automatic routines, allowing our brain to conserve energy and effort. By establishing positive habits, we can streamline our actions, eliminate decision fatigue, and direct our energy towards meaningful tasks. Productive habits create a framework for success, propelling us closer to our goals with consistency and efficiency.

Identifying Key Habits

The first step in harnessing the power of habits for productivity is identifying the key behaviors and routines that align with our goals. Consider activities such as setting specific intentions for each day, prioritizing tasks, breaking projects into smaller, manageable chunks, and dedicating focused time blocks for deep work. By pinpointing these vital habits, we can create a strong foundation for increased productivity.

Building Habits Gradually

Building new habits requires patience and consistency. Instead of attempting to overhaul our entire routine overnight, it is more effective to introduce new habits gradually. Start with one or two key behaviors and commit to practicing them consistently for a significant period, typically around 30 days. Whether it is waking up early, practicing mindfulness, or organizing your workspace, gradually integrating these habits into your daily life allows them to become second nature.

Creating Triggers and Rituals

Triggers and rituals provide cues that prompt our desired habits. For example, if you wish to develop a habit of writing in the morning, designate a specific time and place for writing and gather the necessary tools beforehand. This visual cue will become a trigger for the habit, signaling your brain to shift into writing mode. Rituals, such as lighting a candle or playing calming music, can further enhance focus and signal the start of a productive session.

Overcoming Obstacles

Habits are not immune to challenges and setbacks. Inevitably, we may encounter obstacles that threaten to derail our progress. It is crucial to proactively identify potential barriers and develop strategies to overcome them. Whether it's the temptation of distractions, lack of motivation, or moments of fatigue, having a plan in place to navigate these hurdles ensures that our habits remain intact and our productivity stays on track.

Monitoring and Evaluation

Consistent monitoring and evaluation are essential to maintaining productive habits. Regularly assess your habits' effectiveness and be open to making adjustments when necessary. Stay attuned to the outcome of each habit and its impact on your overall productivity. Celebrate your successes, identify areas for improvement, and remain flexible in adapting your habits to align with your changing goals and lifestyle.

By building positive routines and gradually integrating them into our daily lives, we cultivate a strong foundation for success. Remember, productivity is not about trying to do more in less time, but rather focusing on meaningful tasks, maximizing efficiency, and producing high-quality results. With dedication, consistency, and a commitment to building productive habits, we can unlock our true potential and achieve our goals with ease.

CHAPTER 9. MASTERING DIGITAL DISTRACTIONS

Chances are, you're going to look away in less than a minute. You might get a notification or decide to check social media we all have done this thousands of times. We live in a time where digital distraction is everywhere. We have access to nearly anything and everything we could ever ask for. But we need to ask ourselves, Is this a good thing? is this good for us, for our brains, and our long-term growth?

Even with the recent advancements in technology over the last few decades, our brains haven't changed much. The latest estimates suggest that our modern-day brains haven't changed in over 40,000 years, which is a blink of an eye on the trajectory of life on our planet as we know it.
As a result of this lack of change, our brains haven't been able to adapt to digital distractions–this rapidly changing technology and fast-paced lifestyle–which was created to hijack our brain's neural circuitry by creating continuous stressors that have devastating effects on our overall health.

Digital addiction, also known as internet addiction or technology addiction, is a growing concern in today's society. It refers to excessive, compulsive, and problematic use of digital devices and online activities. Understanding the science behind digital addiction can help individuals recognize its impact and make informed decisions about their technology use.

Research suggests that digital addiction has both psychological and neurological components. Psychologically, the constant availability of online content and social media platforms can trigger a reward system in the brain, leading to cravings and compulsive behavior. The fear of missing out (FOMO), the need for social validation, and the instant gratification provided by technology contribute to the addictive nature of digital devices.

On a neurological level, studies have shown that excessive screen time can alter brain structure and function. The release of dopamine, a neurotransmitter associated with pleasure and reward, plays a significant role in reinforcing digital behaviors. Over time, individuals may develop tolerance, requiring more screen time to experience the same level of satisfaction.

Furthermore, the constant stimulation and multitasking associated with digital devices can negatively affect cognitive processes, such as attention span, memory, and decision-making abilities.

Recognizing the science behind digital addiction underscores the importance of mastering digital detox and establishing healthier relationships with technology.

Social Media and Digital Detox

Social media platforms have become integral parts of our lives, offering opportunities for connection, self-expression, and information sharing. However, excessive use of social media can have negative effects on mental health and well-being. Incorporating digital detox practices specifically targeted at social media can help individuals maintain a healthier relationship with these platforms.

One effective strategy is to set specific time limits for social media use. Designate certain periods of the day for checking and engaging with social media, and outside of those times, commit to staying offline. This approach prevents mindless scrolling and ensures that social media use is intentional and controlled.

Another helpful practice is to curate your social media feed. Unfollow accounts that don't bring you joy, evoke negative emotions, or contribute to comparison and self-doubt. Instead, follow accounts that inspire, educate, and uplift you.

Additionally, consider implementing regular social media detox periods. This can involve taking breaks from social media for a day, a weekend, or even longer. Use this time to focus on activities that bring you fulfillment and allow you to connect with the present moment.

By adopting these strategies, individuals can maintain a healthier balance between social media use and real-life experiences.

So how do we deal with With Digital Distractions?

Here are a few tips to help you effectively deal with digital distractions and improve your focus.

※ Kiss Your Notifications Goodbye

In his hallmark book, Indistractible, author Nir Eyal goes into great detail about how social media companies ingeniously created "alerts" to seduce the mind into spending more time on a platform. Thus, the companies created increasing viewing times, leading to greater revenue and creating a dependency on updated information.

Much like casinos, these tactics heavily involve similar reward pathways within the brain, causing the user to become a dopamine-addicted fiend by using likes, clicks, and alerts to fuel an archaic positive-feedback system that keeps them coming back for more. So, how do you become indistractable?

To start, there's a simple question you need to ask yourself. Do you actually need to know when someone likes a friend's page?

In the grand scheme of things, how impactful is it to see that you got 20 likes on your post from yesterday? And is it going to change your career trajectory if your friend posted a cat video on their TikTok page?

Let's be honest, alerts are nothing more than simple distractions to take you away from the task at hand. So why not just get rid of them?

✻ Embrace StructurePlanning your day
can be one of the most efficient uses of your time. Remember, structure is needed to accomplish your tasks because it allows you greater freedom, more free time, and makes it possible to meet deadlines.

Saving money may not be the most glorious habit. Still, those small habits of saving can compound into significant personal and financial freedoms later in life, essentially allowing you the freedom to retire from work and still have the financial flexibility to continue with life.

The same is true with using social media and digital platforms for enjoyment. Planning the times and duration for using these platforms can be one of the most efficient uses of your time because it creates boundaries.

Remember, influencers on social media platforms don't have enough time in the day to be scrolling and creating content, but they make you feel like they do. This principle is also true for you, especially if you use digital platforms to promote your brand, business, or company.

✻ Use Digital Platforms to Grow, Not to Show
Who you choose to follow on social media will dictate how productive you are when you're not actively scrolling.

Why? Because your newsfeed will influence the emotions, feelings, and reactions to drive you either a step closer or further away from achieving your goals.

When digital distractions become rampant, they take you away from the tasks at hand and can cause you to feel guilty because of how they make you feel. Humans are social animals and can be easily influenced by their surroundings. Case in point: Dr. Stanley Milgram performed multiple studies in the 1960s where participants were asked to induce a graded electric shock to an "unknowingly" willing participant in a separate room.

Over time, the participants were asked to turn up the intensity of the shocks, reaching a point of lethal shock intensity. Even at lethal shock levels, the participants kept inducing shocks to the individual in the closed room per suggestions from the accompanying individual in the room guiding them through the exercise.

Why? Because when people have authority, we inherently obey their orders to feel connected and socially accepted, even if those orders involve drastic actions and near-fatal outcomes.

Luckily, no individuals were harmed during these experiments because the participants in the closed room were actually actors hired to play the part of being shocked.

But this experiment is a powerful lesson for us all: authoritative forces like social media influencers and people with high follower counts have the capacity to change our behaviors.

✱ Choose to Focus, and Your Life Will Come Into Focus
If you've ever been looking for a new car, you know how impactful intentional focus can be on accomplishing a task. It is at this moment when you realize that every other person on the road is driving the same car that you've been looking to buy. How is this possible?

The amount of cars on the road hasn't changed. Your perceptions have. It's always been that way, but once your brain starts to focus on a specific detail, you start seeing more of it manifest throughout your environment. This happens regardless of whether or not you're looking for the good, the bad, or the ugly. What you hope to see is what you will eventually get.

When you focus your time and energy on accomplishing your end task, your brain will find things to reinforce this pattern, thus creating an inevitable positive feedback cycle that will take you and your game to the next level!

CHAPTER 10. BALANCING WORK AND PERSONAL LIFE: CREATING BOUNDARIES

If you believe that there are no clear boundaries between your work and personal responsibilities, and you often feel that you are constantly running and juggling your tasks, which negatively affects the quality of your life, it is time to stop and think about how to solve this problem. Although sometimes it may seem that the pace of life keeps on accelerating, we have to repeat to ourselves again and again that there are only 24 hours a day during which it is necessary for us to fulfill our commitments, rest, eat and exercise to ensure a good quality of life.

Here are some tips on how to spend your time in a quality way so that all areas of your life are balanced.

* Plan your time

Each week, take the time to plan your next week. Every single day of that week. Your weekly plan needs to be realistic and achievable, by calculating the exact time you will spend on each activity. The plan needs to cover all areas of your life and daily activities. Your time formula (when living a quality and balanced life) should look like this: 24 hours - - ? (sleep hours) - -? (commuting to/from work and other activities) - -? (time for personal commitments) - -?(exercising, physical activities) - -? (time for self-care) = ? (time spent on work).

Time for personal commitments includes all the things that are important and necessary to you. Each person puts different things under the said category, for example, time spent with the family, volunteering, community activities, hobbies, etc.

Time spent on self-care should include eating, personal hygiene, dressing yourself, and other personal preparation. Once you can clearly see what your day looks like - divided according to certain activities with a clear amount of time dedicated to each of them, you can move on to an overall weekly plan. Some days may look the same, while others may differ greatly due to the variety of personal commitments. Once it becomes clear what your week looks like and how many hours you actually have for your professional activities, move on to planning your working hours. Try to clearly arrange your tasks and set the amount of time you need to complete each task or activity. It is important to calculate correctly not only the actual time it takes to performance a certain activity, but also the indirect time related to that activity. For example, if you are planning a meeting, it is not enough to simply estimate its duration - you need to add all the time you will spend preparing for it, going to it and coming back from it, as well as resolving the issues addressed during the meeting.

✳ Save time wherever you can

A clear weekly plan will likely enable you to see that you need more time for some of the things you wish to include, however it is physically impossible. There is also a risk that your plan will be very ambitious, without the opportunity to simply have free time for enjoyable activities such as surfing the internet or social networks, chatting with colleagues or people dear to you, etc. In other words, you may be tempted to plan the perfect week, which will be extremely difficult to follow through, because life is so much more colourful and you never know what might distract you from your plan. Therefore, be self-critical and save time wherever you can.

You may be able to postpone some projects or agreements, but given the scale of your more urgent or ongoing work, it is naïve to expect things to go exactly according to your set plan and that you won't need extra time. Your colleagues may be able to help you with some tasks, you just need to ask them or redistribute the tasks with the help of your immediate superior. Perhaps some of your meetings are less important but time consuming, and you can cancel them by discussing the relevant issues over the phone. Perhaps you can remove certain tasks from your plan that don't generate any added value but take a very long time to complete. Try to take a critical look at your plan and adjust it as necessary to create more free time. Also, try to adequately measure your time and take on new commitments or tasks only when you see that you actually have time for them in your weekly plan.

- Keep track of your plan and the actual time of its execution

Take note of how much time it actually takes to perform your planned activities and tasks. For example, you may have planned to take an hour to respond to emails, but it turned out that you need at least two hours when actually performing this task. If there is no way to avoid investing some extra time in a task, you need to adjust your plan to meet your actual time requirements (in other words, reschedule your time). Time management experts recommend using the 80/20 rule, which provides that 20 percent of effort yields 80 percent of results, and the remaining 80 percent of effort yields only 20 percent of results (also called the Pareto principle).

You will help yourself if you accept the truth that you cannot do everything that is expected of you to make everyone around you happy. For example, if you clearly understand that attending a meeting where your participation is not necessary but others would like you to participate would unnecessarily waste too much time. In this case, the right choice would be to apologize to your colleagues for not attending the meeting, and use the saved time on tasks that depend on you directly. You may also notice that you have planned some activities to take a longer time than is actually needed. For example, it may be enough to spend half an hour in a meeting instead of an hour as you initially thought, and in that case, by leaving earlier, you can invest the time saved in another task that will generate more value for you. Even if some of your decisions may not appeal to others, short-term discomfort and setting clear boundaries can bring more benefits in the long run.

* Seek help

If you have tried applying the first three tips but are still unable to do everything that you have planned for yourself - do not be afraid to ask for help. Before doing so, carefully review your schedule once again and identify the objective reasons why some tasks were not completed. It may not be a matter of your personal planning skills, perhaps you simply have too many work commitments or too many tasks assigned to you. Here are a few things to look for before talking to your immediate superior or colleagues who are trying to give you new tasks:

Gather the facts. Make a clear list of all the tasks and the time required to complete them (if you followed the previous tips, you already know this information).

Visualize your daily, weekly, or longer plan. You can simply print a calendar or visualize the plan in another format. In this case, the form in which you provide the information is less important than its content. Your goal is to clearly show that you do not have enough time to carry out the tasks that you are expected to perform.

Present your information. In this case, the more important thing is not to "prove your truth", but to show the actual situation and ask for help in solving your problem, prioritizing your tasks, delegating them to other team members, simplifying them, etc.

* Review your plans periodically

Take some time to carefully review your plans. It is unlikely that once a perfect plan is put together, it will always fit. You will find that sometimes weekly reviews are enough, but there are times when you need to do your reviews on a daily basis as well. You will eventually get used to estimating the time it takes to perform certain tasks quite accurately, which will allow you to manage and plan your time more effectively.

Don't worry if there are moments throughout the process when you feel bad about not being able to plan everything smoothly. Be patient to yourself and realistic regarding your actual limits. Along the way, you will probably need to learn to say no more often when newly assigned tasks or activities clearly do not fit into your time budget.

CHAPTER 11. THE ART OF SAYING NO: SETTING HEALTHY BOUNDARIES

Do you struggle with asserting yourself and setting limits with others? Here are some ways to create better, stronger boundaries in your life...

'No.'

It is a simple, powerful and necessary word. So why are so many of us afraid of saying it?

And when we do manage to say it, why is this so often followed by a wave of guilt, shame and fear? For instance, guilt that you let someone down. Shame that you aren't a saint or superhero who can help everyone all the time. Fear that you may have damaged or even lost a relationship.

Or maybe the last time you said 'no' to someone, you got a negative response? Maybe they went into a huff, gave you the silent treatment or tried to change your mind? And maybe you dread that ever happening again?

With all the unpleasant emotions and reactions that saying 'no' can create, it's no wonder that it can feel so much easier to agree to everything, whether it suits us or not.

'Yes, I'll work overtime this weekend.'
'Yes, you can borrow more money off me.'

'Yes, I'll babysit again tonight.'
'Yes, I'll take care of your three hyperactive dogs for a fortnight while you're in the Maldives.'
And yet when we refuse to ever refuse people the effect on our wellbeing can be devastating, leading to frustration, burnout and even breakdowns. What's more, we might find that our relationships become rocky or broken.

Of course, there is nothing wrong with helping others out, lending a listening ear or offering support in emergencies. But if you feel that your 'yes' is out of control (while your 'no' is quivering at the back of your sock drawer, afraid to ever come out), then you might just have a problem with boundaries.

Signs of boundary issues

Boundary crossing isn't just about your time, attention and energy, it can show up in many different ways. If someone devalues your emotions, they have violated a boundary. If they pry into your private business, they have violated a boundary. And if they speak to you inappropriately, they have violated a boundary. A boundary is any line that is crossed, whatever that line might be.
With this in mind, can you relate to any of the following?

* You struggle with saying 'no' – and feel guilty when you do so.

- You worry that if you refuse a request you might damage or lose a relationship.
- You often feel that you don't have enough hours in the day.
- You find some of your relationships challenging, draining or dramatic.
- You often feel depleted or overwhelmed.
- You like to please people and be obliging – sometimes at your own expense.
- You feel that people don't respect you.
- You prefer to show your anger and frustration in indirect ways.
- You sometimes overshare – and people overshare with you too.
- You are the person that everyone turns to in emergencies.
- You feel that people don't listen to you.
- You have frequent fantasies of running away from it all.
- You feel that you have to answer texts and calls immediately.
- You feel like you are losing sight of your own hobbies, passions and goals.

Unsurprisingly, weak boundaries can lead to mental and physical health issues such as depression, anxiety and fatigue, which is why it's crucial to put strong ones in place. In fact, healthy limits are probably as essential to our wellbeing as taking vitamins and drinking water.

But how do you go about creating them? And how do you communicate them to others, especially when they might have become very used to hearing 'yes' from you?

So what are boundaries anyway?

Before we answer these questions, it might be helpful to examine what boundaries are in the first place – and what they're not.

First of all, a boundary is not a rigid and intimidating ice fortress that you place between yourself and others. It is not about shutting people out, nor is it somehow 'cold', 'uncaring' or 'rude'. And despite the title of this blog post, a boundary is not always about saying 'no' either – at times, it might actually about be saying 'yes' but selectively and with conditions in place ('Yes, you can borrow my car, but only if you return it with a full tank).

Put simply, a boundary is just a limit that you set in your relationships and then communicate to others. And this limit could be around time, money, privacy, touch, belongings, behaviour, communications or anything at all that matters to you. So for instance, you could create a boundary that the next time you lend your friend money, you will set a date for when you expect to be paid back. Or tell your brother that you can only babysit for him once a month and no more. Or decide that you are no longer going to answer personal questions from strangers about your age, salary or when you plan to have children.

Boundaries are a way to practice self-care, honour your feelings and protect yourself from harm. They are also a way to respect yourself and show the world that you expect respect. In the words of therapist and author Nedra Glover Tawwab, 'A boundary is a cue to others about how to treat you.'

But if you're not sure where the boundary issues are in your life, then pay attention to the times when you feel frustrated, angry, exhausted, overwhelmed or anxious (or just want to escape or hide away). Often, those feelings indicate that you lack healthy limits with a certain situation or person.

People can lack boundaries for all sorts of reasons yet very often, the roots lie in childhood. According to a 2020 article by Boundaries authors Dr. Henry Cloud and Dr. John Townsend, 'Adults with boundary problems…had learned patterns early in life and then continued those out-of-control patterns in their adult lives, where the stakes were higher.'

For instance, if one of your parents had a disability, mental health issue or addiction and needed your support as a child, then you might often find yourself in a helper or rescuer role in adulthood. Or if a caregiver didn't respect your privacy or space (for instance, by going through your things or coming into your room without knocking), then you may not feel that you have a right to privacy as a grownup.

Or if you experienced abuse, neglect or abandonment, then you might still find it hard to assert yourself, because you were taught for so long that your feelings didn't matter. What's more, you may feel so terrified of being abandoned or rejected again that saying 'no' becomes almost impossible.

There is also a gender element to boundaries. For instance, there can still be an expectation in our society for women to be caring, helpful and self-sacrificing, and to carry out the bulk of the 'emotional labour'. For this reason, many women believe that setting limits with others is selfish, wrong or even impossible.

Also, if a person suffers from societal discrimination or is somehow isolated and marginalised, then they might let themselves be taken advantage of so that they can be accepted and liked.

Whatever the reason for having weak boundaries, the good news is that you can learn to strengthen them. In fact, like most things in life, it's just a matter of practice and persistence.

Seven tips for creating healthy boundaries

Unfortunately, a boundary isn't something you can just keep in your head in the hope that everyone will magically know about it. Like it or not you have to express it to others, otherwise how will they even know it exists?

However, it's also possible to set boundaries politely, respectfully and lovingly – and by doing so, your relationships can become healthier as there will be much less room for simmering resentments. As Brené Brown points out in The Gifts of Imperfection, 'When we fail to set boundaries and hold people accountable, we feel used and mistreated.'

And while you might experience feelings of guilt or unease at first, the more you practice your 'no' the easier it will become to say it (and the more others will get used to hearing it too).

There are various ways to communicate boundaries, depending on the situation and relationship. Here are a few tips for how to do so effectively:

❋ State your feelings and set limits

Explain calmly how a particular behaviour affects you, then follow this by putting a clear boundary in place.

For instance, 'When you make jokes about my weight, I feel terrible. Please stop.' Continue to repeat this as often as you need to until the person gets the message, but remember to keep your cool while doing so. If they refuse to stop, then it is possible that the relationship is bullying or abusive and you may need to seek support.

※ Be short and to the point
If you set a boundary in a way that's overly complex or convoluted, then people might not even understand what you're saying at all. While it's fine to want to be polite, subtlety can sometimes be the enemy of being heard.
So aim to keep it simple, beginning with statements like 'I'd like…', 'I need…' or 'I expect'. This has the benefit of being straightforward and also keeps the focus on you instead of the other person, meaning that they are less likely to feel attacked.

※ Never apologise
It's all too easy to feel that every 'no' must be followed with a 'sorry', but that's not the case at all. You have a right to your boundaries and don't need to apologise for them. In fact, saying 'sorry' can sometimes weaken the effect of setting a limit, as it suggests that you think you are doing something wrong.

Instead, aim for polite but firm statements like: 'Thanks for the invite, that sounds like fun but I'm not free.'

✳ Don't let people poke holes in your 'no'
If you find it hard to refuse people, then you might feel you have to offer detailed explanations for doing so. But the problem is that when you over-explain, people can use it as a way to find weaknesses in your boundary. So don't say, 'Thanks for inviting me to your party, but I can't make it as I'm not drinking alcohol right now for health reasons, you know?' If you say this, then you run the risk of your friend promising to make you tasty mocktails and nagging you until you change your mind.
Instead say, 'Thanks for inviting me to your party, but I can't make it.' It's not necessary to explain why you can't make it. If the person pushes you for more details then you don't have to give them, however if you decide to, keep it short and sweet.

✳ Be resilient to guilt trips and manipulation
There might be some people in your life who simply can't handle the word 'no'. They might needle and wheedle until they get their way, throw tantrums, give you the silent treatment or just ignore your boundary altogether.
If this happens, remind yourself that boundaries help to keep relationships healthy, so you will both benefit from having them in place. It's also worth remembering that people can take time to get used to new boundaries and

might test them for a while, especially if they are very close to you.

However, if you feel that you are struggling to maintain boundaries with certain individuals then you might benefit from talking to a therapist about this.

�֍ Get comfortable with negative emotions

Stating boundaries – especially when you're not used to doing so – can bring up feelings of guilt, fear, shame, panic, unease, sadness or awkwardness. Learn to expect this as a natural part of setting new limits in relationships, rather than as a sign that you were 'wrong' to put one there. If it helps, you could create rituals for processing any feelings that come up, such as meditation, journalling or simply going for a long walk.

�֍ Create consequences for boundary violations

For instance, 'From now on, if you raise your voice at me on the phone, I will hang up' or 'If you don't pay me back the money on the date we have agreed on, I won't be able to lend you any more in future'.

However, it's important that you follow through with your promises or your boundary won't get taken seriously. Also, accept that you might have to uphold your limit several times until the person gets the message, especially if their problem behaviour is longstanding. Sometimes, it just takes patience, persistence and resilience. Remember that if someone crosses a clear boundary then this is their responsibility, not yours, so they will have to deal with any consequences.

Learning to set limits with people isn't easy, so try not to be too hard on yourself if you don't do it 'perfectly' at first. Also, don't be surprised if you get a bit of pushback, feel overwhelmed with guilt or find yourself apologising. Like any other interpersonal skill this is something that you will refine over time. But it's all well worth it as when you develop stronger boundaries, your life starts to thrive. For instance, you might feel less burned out, have more time for your passions and just communicate better in general.

Boundaries are about having your needs honored by others, but they are also about honouring your own needs. So while setting healthy limits can improve your relationships, remember that by practicing the art of saying 'no', you can also improve your relationship with yourself.

CHAPTER 12. NURTURING SELF-CARE AND WELLNESS IN YOUR ROUTINE

Self-care is not just a luxury; it is a vital practice that helps us maintain balance and enhance our overall well-being. By prioritizing self-care rituals, we can nurture our mental and physical health, promoting a sense of calm, rejuvenation, and self-love. In this blog post, we'll explore some effective self-care rituals that you can incorporate into your daily routine to enhance your well-being.

Are you ready to embark on a transformative journey towards self-care? Picture yourself feeling revitalized, balanced, and more connected with your own well-being.

※ Decoding Self-Care

According to leading psychologists and researchers, self-care is a deliberate practice of nurturing your overall well-being. It involves prioritizing your own needs and intentionally engaging in activities that promote physical, mental, and emotional health. Self-care encompasses various aspects of life, including nutrition, exercise, relaxation, mindfulness, and personal growth. By dedicating time and attention to yourself, you cultivate a foundation of self-love and self-respect.

Consider this: What does self-care mean to you?

Take a moment to reflect on your understanding of self-care and how it currently shows up in your life.

Are there areas where you can enhance your self-care practices?

✷ The Physical Benefits

Engaging in regular self-care activities can have a profound impact on your physical well-being. When you prioritize physical self-care, you make choices that nourish your body and support its optimal functioning. This may involve adopting a balanced and nutritious diet, engaging in regular exercise, getting enough sleep, and tending to your body's needs. Scientific studies have shown that practicing self-care has been associated with improved physical health outcomes.

Let's consider the physical self-care practices that resonate with you.

How can you incorporate more movement, nutritious foods, and restful sleep into your daily routine?

What small steps can you take today to prioritize your physical well-being?

✷ The Mental and Emotional Benefits

Self-care is equally essential for your mental and emotional well-being. Taking time to nurture your mind and emotions can significantly impact your overall quality of life. Engaging in activities that reduce stress, enhance mood, and promote emotional resilience are key components of mental and emotional self-care. This may involve practicing mindfulness, engaging in creative outlets, setting boundaries, seeking support, and practicing self-compassion. Research has shown that self-care practices can contribute to increased happiness and life satisfaction.

In practice, self-care is multifaceted. "The way I define self-care is the intentional, proactive pursuit of integrated wellness that balances mind, body, and spirit personally and professionally," Just eating healthy isn't enough anymore, things are moving so fast around us that we need space to self-care and slow down to rest from all the busyness in our lives.
Just because a behavior is good for you, that doesn't make it self-care. I recommend finding something you look forward to for self-care, that might be something that supports physical health, like a certain type of exercise, or something that's purely for joy, like a massage or regular dinners with friends.
The common denominator of self-care practices is that you get some enjoyment out of the activity.

Need some inspiration for how you can find your moment of zen? Here are some easy ideas to include in your Self Care Routine.

Create Calm
Set a calm, peaceful atmosphere. Scent has a powerful effect on our sense of wellbeing. Pop some essential oil in a diffuser to create a soothing environment. Or place a few drops of oil in the palm of your hand, then inhale deeply.

Soft lighting, such as a lamp or candlelight promotes a relaxing space.
Play some gentle music, or a guided meditation to signal to yourself you are ready to quieten and unwind.

✳ Immerse yourself in water

Water is beneficial in so many ways. If short on time, why not make yourself, or your children a foot bath? Add Epsom or Magnesium Salts which are easily absorbed through the feet.
Or run yourself a relaxing bath. Add salts, oil or a bundle of your favourite herbs to really enhance your experience.
A saltwater swim, though still bracing at this time of year, cleanses and refreshes your energy. You'll feel amazing afterwards and totally revitalised.

✳ Walk with mindfulness

Take a nature walk. Observe things you haven't noticed before. Spring bulbs and blossoms ready to bloom or birds tending to their nests. Deeply inhale as you walk. Feel the benefits of oxygen reaching new places within your body. Swing your arms as you move. If possible, remove your shoes and feel the earth under your feet. This will replenish and restore your energy.

✳ Be tech free

Try a technology-free afternoon. Or put your phone on silent after 7pm. We forgot how easily we are pulled into public space from within our homes. Create boundaries around when you choose to be available to others. Notice how you feel in response to creating more space.

※ Food for thought
Make yourself a delicious meal. Take time as you prepare it. Fully savour the tactile and sensory qualities of your food. Smell each ingredient before you prepare it. Chop things in a new way. Serve your meal in a special dish. Eat your meal slowly and mindfully.

CHAPTER 13. IGNITING PASSION AND FINDING PURPOSE

In the pursuit of a meaningful and fulfilling life, it's essential to embrace your passions and align them with a greater purpose. By pursuing your passions and living a purpose-driven life, you can experience a profound sense of joy, fulfillment, and authenticity.

If you want to experience true happiness, joy, and personal fulfillment in life, look in the direction of your passion and purpose. For most people, these two often take the back seat because of the need for survival–working around the clock to pay the bills and live a good life.

However, when you think long rather than short, you will find that nothing else satisfies the deep-seated longing in every person for fulfillment other than living purposefully and exercising their true passion. This article focuses on how you can connect your passion and purpose to find fulfillment in life.

How to Connect Your Passion With Purpose

* Discovering Your Passion
* Discovering Your Purpose
* Connecting Passion With Purpose

Passion Vs Purpose

While the two are inextricably connected, they are also distinct entities and should be understood apart as well as together.

What Is Passion?

Passion is what releases your emotions, what motivates you, and what makes you feel good. Passion is often connected to your innate abilities, talent, and desires. It is what you love to do and do well without feeling stressed or compelled.

Passion is an essential ingredient for success. Most successful people are people of great passion. When you have passion for something, you will strive towards its mastery, and this boosts your productivity. Passion also boosts your confidence, and confidence leads to success. With passion, you can muscle the required strength to forge through life challenges and other hurdles that stop others from becoming successful.

What Is Purpose?

Purpose is the reason you do what you do. It is the motivation behind your actions and pursuits in life. Purpose is often connected to an understanding of a reason for living–the reason behind your unique life story, your background, and the future ahead of you.

Purpose is very important in life; it is actually the true yardstick for measuring success and impact. Purpose gives your life a direction and keeps you focused. When you know the reason why you are who you are and what you are meant to do, your life ceases to be an experiment; rather you will be living with conviction, and life becomes more meaningful.

The Differences

There are key differences between passion and purpose, although you should bring them together to live a fulfilled life. Purpose is based on conviction, while passion is based on energy, feeling, and interest. Passion can burn out over time. However, purpose is for a lifetime.

Passion is about "what," and purpose is about "why." You can be passionate about different things, but purpose is usually singular and focused.
The challenge with most people is that their passion and purpose are disjointed. Some do not even have any conviction for living and only live for the moment. Others deploy their passion for the wrong things, and when passion is not connected with purpose, it eventually leads to burnout. This is why people lose enthusiasm when they face a major life crisis. But when your passion is connected to a purpose, you will record extraordinary results in your life.

Think about lighting a fire; passion is the fuel required to make the fire burn, while purpose is the reason the fire is lit –what you want to achieve by kindling the fire. When you have the conviction to spark a fire, your passion is ignited and your entire energy is released. This is why it is essential for your passion and purpose to work together.
Before you can connect your passion with purpose, you have to first identify what your passions are and what your purpose is. Below are some guides on discovering your passion and purpose.

In order to discover your passion, you have to pay attention to yourself. This is because your passion stems from your expressions. The following are some questions to ask yourself to know what your true passion is:

- What things do I do that give me joy?
- Which subjects interest me to learn and learn more?
- What job/work can I volunteer to do for a long time without financial reward?
- What would I use my time for if I could do what I like and still get paid?
- What makes me feel "in the zone"? What do I do very skillfully, easily, and delightfully?

When you have discovered your passion, the next thing is to find out what your purpose is so that you can begin to channel your passion in the direction of your purpose.

Purpose actually precedes passion, though we often get to discover our passions first because they are expressive. Your passions can be a clue to help you figure out what your purpose is. You can ask yourself some questions to have an idea of your purpose.

Using our fuel-fire example, it can be asked: Why do I have a fuel? Is there a need for a fire? And if there is a need for a fire, what is it meant to burn? More practically, you can ask:

* Why do I have this gift?
* Why do I have that talent?
* Why is it so easy for me to do this while I struggle to do other things?
* Why do issues like these bother me when I don't care about some other issues?
* Why am I experiencing this in my life?
* What are my past and present experiences saying about my future?

The issue of purpose might require some deep soul searching and possibly divine inspiration. One of the proofs you have found your purpose is strong conviction. This is what makes you become resolute, ready, and willing to commit yourself to a life-long assignment.

To start connecting your passion with purpose, the following are practical suggestions to consider:

* Examine your life

In whatever stage of life that you are, you can re-examine your life and journey. Do a soul-search on what your true passion and purpose are. This may require that you take time out of your current schedules and retreat to a place where you can focus only on yourself. You can plan this for your next holiday.

You can also start by reading more on the subjects of passion and purpose to prepare your mind and guide you in your self-evaluation.

✳ Begin to live with conviction

When you have figured out what your passion and purpose are, let it reflect in your life. Begin to live every day with your new conviction. Let it reflect in how you spend your time, what you read about, what you talk about, and what you devote yourself to. Begin to see things in your life through the lens of your conviction.

You'll also begin to consider how you can use your daily encounters to keep yourself in the direction of your conviction.

✳ Redirect your passion

To connect your passion with purpose, you might have to begin to redirect your passion. This is because you might have been using your energy and abilities on the wrong things. But when you have figured out why you have those energies, desires, and interests as earlier mentioned, then you should redirect your passion towards your conviction.

※ Embrace new opportunities
What you are currently involved in probably does not represent your true passion and purpose at all. It might be your job or chosen career, things you've spent a good part of your years pursuing and developing. You may not have to quit those things, but you can look for new opportunities to express your true passion and purpose.

※ Make major adjustments
To really experience fulfillment in life, you might need to make major adjustments. This might affect your current career path or whatever else you are involved in. There is no price that is too much to pay to earn yourself the kind of life that you truly deserve. You don't have to continue to be what the "system" has made you be when you know that it won't lead to where you truly belong.

A whole lot changes in life when you identify your true passion and discover your purpose. It gets more beautiful when you are able to connect your passion with your purpose. Your life will be more meaningful, rewarding, impactful, and fulfilling. You will be proud to be alive, knowing that your energies are being applied in the right direction.

Your true purpose offers you an unmistakable sense of joy, freedom, and hope. It lights you up inside and sparks a desire for more in-depth exploration into the unknown.

CHAPTER 14. CULTIVATING A POSITIVE MINDSET FOR SUCCESS

To cultivate a positive mindset, it is important to start by examining our thoughts and beliefs. Identifying negative thought patterns and consciously reframing them into more positive and empowering ones can significantly impact our mindset. By challenging self-limiting beliefs and replacing them with affirming thoughts, we can create a more positive internal dialogue.

Practicing gratitude is another powerful tool for cultivating a positive mindset. Taking time each day to reflect on things we are grateful for can shift our focus from negativity to appreciation, enhancing our overall well-being. Gratitude journaling and expressing appreciation to others are effective ways to incorporate gratitude into our daily lives.

Let's take a deeper look into gratitude.

One of the most powerful ways to cultivate a positive mindset is to focus on gratitude. Take a few minutes each day to reflect on the things in your life that you are grateful for, whether it's your health, your family, your job, or simply the beauty of nature. By focusing on the positive aspects of your life, you can shift your mindset from one of negativity and stress to one of gratitude and positivity.

Whatever your circumstances in life, you may find that consistently showing gratitude can be surprisingly difficult. Many of us get caught up in a negativity bias, where we linger on bad news and unpleasant experiences, yet allow moments of positivity to fade into the background.

Maybe you spend so much time dreading work on Monday that you don't take time to fully appreciate the weekend. Or perhaps you're so focused on your own verbal slip-up at a party that you don't register a compliment from a friend. And if you have a mood disorder such as depression, being able to see any positives or express gratitude can seem impossible.

Fortunately, gratitude is like a muscle that you can build. With the right exercises and practice, you can find at least something small to appreciate in even the bleakest day. The idea of cultivating gratitude might sound cheesy, but research has shown that it can have very real benefits. These benefits include;

- Better sleep.
- Improved focus.
- Higher self-esteem.
- Increased patience.

For some of us, gratitude seems to come naturally. You might already have a grateful disposition, which leads you to look for and cherish the good in life. On the other hand, certain personality traits and mood disorders can act as barriers to being able to acknowledge and express gratitude.

Here are a few factors that can fuel your negativity bias:

- Envy. If you desire another person's traits or possessions, you may feel unhappy if a friend has found more success in dating or bitter that a coworker received a promotion you believe you deserve. It's easy to become so wrapped up in envy that you overlook your own fortunes.

- Materialism. If you're materialistic, you hold the belief that having more possessions will eventually lead to happiness. Maybe you believe that you need the latest gadgets to impress your friends or maintain a certain social status. Or perhaps you think that a large house and fancy car will make you happy. Rather than being grateful for what you have, you're always looking for new things to claim as your own.

- Cynicism. If you're cynical, you tend to believe that people only act within their own self-interests. You might believe that someone gave you a gift just because they want a favor in return. This mindset makes it hard to feel gratitude toward other people.

- Narcissism. People who are narcissistic tend to be self-centered and have an excessive need for admiration. Narcissists also tend to have a sense of entitlement.

They're prone to overlooking gifts and good fortune because they expect favorable treatment.

* Stress. The general stressors of everyday life can loom so large that you have a hard time seeing the blessings around you. You might want to feel grateful for having a place to live, but the stress of keeping up with bills is always at the forefront of your mind.

* Depression. Depression is more complicated than just feeling sad. It can involve a deep sense of despair and hopelessness that leaves you feeling fatigued, isolated, and empty. You might imagine it as a veil that obscures all the positive aspects of your life.

Factors like envy and materialism can lead you to take things for granted. But if you can acknowledge the good in your own life—whether it's a roof over your head, reliable friends, or good health—you can avoid comparing your own life to other people's lives.

If you're feeling stressed or depressed, positivity is often hard to come by. However, even on the worst days, if you look hard enough you can usually find at least one thing to be grateful about. Keep an eye out for small moments of pleasure—the smell of good food, playtime with a pet, or a catchy tune on the radio. Noticing even the tiniest glimmers of positivity can make a big difference in your day.

So how do we build the gratitude muscle–and become more appreciative? Here are some simple strategies:

- Begin and end with intention. Start each day by thinking about all you appreciate and expect from the day, and as you turn out the lights at the end of each day also consider all you're grateful for.

- Give continuous attention. Throughout each day, find small things about which you can be thankful. Perhaps the line at the coffee place was shorter this morning or your coworker made you smile. Avoid taking things for granted. Make everything count and bring conscious attention to elements which make you glad.

- Be expansive. Ensure you're focusing on being grateful not just for things, but for people and conditions. Perhaps you particularly appreciate the headphones which help make your workout more fun, but also pay attention to the person at the club who made you feel welcome or the fact that you have the capability to walk, lift or stretch.

- Write it down. Research at Kent State University found when you write down elements you're grateful for, that simple act can foster happiness and wellbeing. This is probably true because it causes you to pause, focus, reflect and reinforce your positive experiences.

* Express yourself. Gratitude is both an individual and a team sport. When you share what you're grateful for in a team environment, it holds even more power. Thank a coworker during a team meeting or provide positive feedback to a colleague during a project session. When gratitude is expressed and shared, it helps both you and the group.

CHAPTER 15. OWNING YOUR TIME: CREATING A WEEKLY REVIEW PROCESS

All too often, we get so tied up in keeping on top of smaller tasks that we forget to look at the bigger picture. Then, before you know it, weeks have passed and you realize you've spent more time responding to tasks than you have done choosing them.

Weekly reviews are a great opportunity just to stop, pause, and take stock of where you are and where you're headed. Whether you follow a formal, step-by-step guide, as per David Allen's famous Getting Things Done method, or you just set a reminder on your phone to spend a few minutes reflecting on what's happening in your life each week, conducting a weekly review can help you get more control over your to-do list – and your life. Here's how to get started.

What is a weekly review?

A study from Harvard Business School reveals we learn better when we reflect. The same goes for achieving your goals: Reflection is key to moving forward with purpose.

* There are several variations on the weekly review, but essentially, it's all about reflection – on the week that's been, the week ahead, and the weeks beyond. Some reviews include detailed steps, whereas others consist of

a few pertinent questions. At their essence, they cover the following ground:
* What goals do I need to accomplish next week?
* How can I improve on what I'm doing?
* What big picture things would I like to work toward?

When it comes to reviews, they can be any unit of time apart, but a week seems to work best. It's regular, but not so frequent that it takes up too much time. Most of us work in weeks, too; Monday to Friday is a big part of traditional workplace culture. Incorporating a review into an already established pattern makes it easier to turn it into a routine.

Who should do a weekly review?

Short answer: everyone. It's such a useful trick, and it only takes an hour. And, when you think about how many hours there are in a week, sacrificing one to get more out of the rest sounds like a pretty good deal.
If any of the below questions sound like you, then a weekly review is definitely something you should consider.

* I get to the end of the week/month/year and have no idea what I've actually done.
* I start each day without a plan and just do tasks as they come in.
* I feel incredibly busy, but I'm not reaching my goals.
* I want to be more productive in general.

- I want more time set aside to focus on self-improvement and personal development.
- I feel like I'm only just keeping my head above water each day.
- I don't feel fulfilled.

There are lots of benefits to a weekly review, but here are two of the biggest.

Learn more about yourself

All too easily, we get tied up in deadlines and emails and forget what really matters to us. The best thing about a weekly review is the opportunity to reflect. And, after doing it a few weeks in a row, you'll start to spot patterns you may not have noticed otherwise.

For example, if you missed deadlines because you kept getting distracted by messages on chat, you could make it a priority to only check-in at certain times during the day, allowing more time for deep focus. Or perhaps you noticed you consistently get more done in the mornings than you do in the afternoons. Armed with that information, you can structure your day around your own productivity peaks and dips. As a result, you'll make more informed decisions and ultimately get more done in less time.

Continually improve

If you run a 5k every day and never time it, you'll never know if you're doing any better or worse than the last time.

The same goes for work: The best way to get better is to measure and track your progress.

Begin by choosing some metrics to measure. These could be anything, from words written per hour to the number of Pomodoros completed. Eventually, you'll reach a point where your progress plateaus. But, if you keep measuring, it's easier to stay on your A-game and not let things slip.

Here's how to start your weekly review.

✳ **Choose a time to do your weekly review**
The day you pick is up to you, but we recommend Friday afternoons: It's when the week's drawing to a close and our concentration dips. Completing a weekly review is a great way to fill time. It also means that when you start work on Monday, you know right away what you need to do. Sunday is another good option because you can channel your nervous 'work tomorrow' energy into something productive.

Really, it doesn't matter when it is, but it should be the same time every week. Eventually, you'll do it enough times that it'll become second nature.

✳ **Tidy up and clear out**
A clear space really does help you focus – so tidy everything around you, sort through any stray pieces of paper, declutter your inbox (but don't worry too much about inbox zero), organize your chats into specific topics, and generally have a physical, mental, and digital clear-out.

This helps you feel calm, organized, and ready to think about your goals.

✳︎ Create a set of weekly review questions

These should be the same each week. You can tailor these to suit your needs, but below are some core questions. Write down your answers, and use them to plan your week ahead.

- ✳︎ What deadlines, projects, and tasks do I have coming up?
- ✳︎ Am I keeping up with my obligations?
- ✳︎ What went well this past week? How can I make sure more good stuff happens again?
- ✳︎ Did anything go badly last week? How can I stop that from happening again?
- ✳︎ What are my goals for next week?
- ✳︎ What are my goals for the next month? Quarter? Year?

Is everything I'm doing helping me reach my goals?

What can I do about the things that aren't?

Be pragmatic. As much as we all want to be one of those people who gets up at sunrise, runs a 10k, and has completed half their to-do list by 8 a.m., it's just not that realistic. When creating your weekly review, start with small steps, and build on those gradually.

✳︎ Review your answers

Check your weekly review does what it needs to do. Here are some good questions to ask yourself:

- Does it guide me through the week ahead?
- Does it help me assess the past week?
- Have I included time to organize and declutter?
- Is there room to pause and evaluate my major goals?
- Is there space to reflect on where I am and where I'm heading?
- Have I given myself time to step back and work on personal projects?

Next, post a review: Be kind to yourself.

When you look back at your day, week, or month and realize you've not met as many goals as you'd have liked, it's easy to beat yourself up. But remember: this is the reason you're doing the weekly review – to see how you're doing and improve. Measuring your progress is part of improving, so even acknowledging slip-ups and inefficiency is a step in the right direction.

Below is the Weekly Review method by- David Allen. It's an impactful practice for those who practice GTD, but it's also a key component of other popular productivity methods like time blocking and OKRs. The truth is everyone should do a weekly review regardless of their day-to-day workflow. There's no one-size-fits-all method, so customize your weekly review to work for you.

THE WEEKLY REVIEW

0 - 10 MINUTES
Declutter & mind dump

Tidy your workspace, file away your notes, and get all your tasks out of your head and into your task management system.

10 - 20 MINUTES
Reflect on the past week

Review your completed tasks, calendar, notes and goals. Compare your plan to what actually happened. What went well? What didn't?

20 - 35 MINUTES
Get current on goals & projects

What progress have you made on each of your top priorities? What needs to be updated? What needs to happen next?

35 - 50 MINUTES
Plan the week ahead

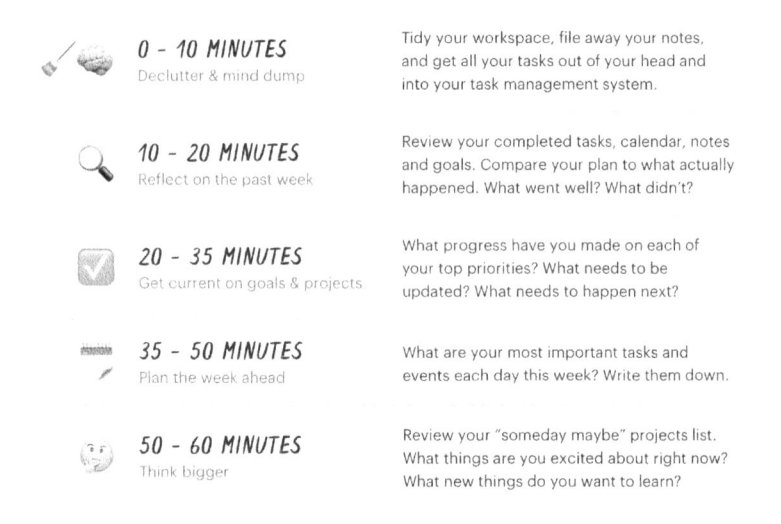

What are your most important tasks and events each day this week? Write them down.

50 - 60 MINUTES
Think bigger

Review your "someday maybe" projects list. What things are you excited about right now? What new things do you want to learn?

"The Weekly Review will sharpen your intuitive focus on your important projects as you deal with the flood of new input and potential distractions coming at you the rest of the week." David Allen, Getting Things Done.

CHAPTER 16. SUSTAINING MOTIVATION: MOMENTUM FOR THE LONG RUN.

According to physics, a body in motion stays in motion, and a body at rest stays at rest. Therefore, if you want lasting success, it's critical to keep building momentum to push towards your goals.

Many people are motivated for short bursts of time and then find that their motivation wanes. One only has to look at the increased attendance at fitness clubs each January and then return a few months later to see that many people have not been able to stick to their New Year's resolution fitness goals. Success is not achieved within periods of fleeting motivation. Goals, dreams, and long-term successes are only achieved while staying motivated for long periods of time. Our ability and desire to get up day after day to pursue our dreams is what separates those of us with high levels of motivation from those who only have fleeting commitment. The key distinction between sustained and fleeting motivation is disciplined effort. Motivation does not sustain itself. Those who relentlessly pursue their goals and dreams with focused discipline and ambitious effort are the people who obtain sustained motivation. When we give more disciplined effort, we will feel more motivation.

The secret of success is learning how to use pain and pleasure instead of having pain and pleasure use you. If you do that, you're in control of your life. If you don't, life controls you.
- Tony Robbins

In the classic book, Think and Grow Rich, Napoleon Hill tells the story of Edwin C. Barnes, the man who would eventually become a long-time business partner of Thomas Edison.

Barnes gave up everything for a chance to partner with Edison and left his life at the time behind for a chance to get close to the famous inventor. Over the course of years and through sheer dedication, Barnes eventually inked an incredibly lucrative business relationship with Edison that made him both wealthy and fulfilled, having accomplished his one burning desire.

That kind of dedication is rare, and maintaining the motivation necessary to pursue such a goal can seem quite difficult. So, what's the secret? The book suggests that there's magic in having a burning desire and that, in order to cultivate that you need to get crystal clear on your goal by writing it down, being specific, and reading it daily. However, I'd argue that there's a missing layer to that which is critical to maintaining the motivation necessary to achieve any long-term goal.

So what motivates us (and why we lose it)

At the heart of motivation exists the desire to do something. If it weren't for the desire to do something, there would be no need for motivation. This is why you're doing what you're doing, why you "need" motivation in the first place.

It goes without saying, then, that you need to get clear on why you want what you want. If you can get clear on why you're doing something, why you want something, and remind yourself daily, you'll clear away much of the resistance you have towards taking action. The opposite is true as well. If you stop reminding yourself why you're taking action, what your goals are, and why they're important? You lose your motivation.

However, this is just a mechanism to help get us to act, it's not usually enough to spur us to action, especially when you're already lacking motivation. For that, we need to know why we act one way vs. another in the first place.

* Why do you reach for those M&Ms when you should be making yourself a salad?
* Why do you sleep in instead of getting up to exercise? And why don't you just walk into your boss's office to ask for a raise?

If you're familiar with Tony Robbins' work, you'll recognize the phrase pain and pleasure. Robbins talks about it often (and he got it from Freud), and it's the key to understanding why we do what we do. You might be very clear on what you want to accomplish, but if the pain (in your mind) associated with taking action on that goal is greater than the pleasure of accomplishing it, then you won't take action.

If you can get good at generating empowering-pleasurable-emotions and connect them to accomplishing your long-term goal, you can use them at will to override the immediate pain of the negative emotions associated with taking action now (be it the fear of "what will my boss say to me," or the discomfort of forcing yourself up in the morning and feeling tired). And you'll be far more likely to take action.

Let's do a little exercise, this is intended to help you begin generating a more resilient, pure motivation utilizing what we've talked about thus far, with empowering emotions and the play between pain and pleasure. The more you use it, the more powerful it is, so make it a point to stick to it for a few weeks straight to grow accustomed to doing it daily.

Take our a pen and paper or use a journal.

1. Write down your goal (Get crystal clear)

It's important to be crystal clear and very specific about your goal (or goals) when you write it down. If your goal is to exercise more:

- How many days a week?
- How long is each session?

- From what date to what date? (even if you plan on continuing past the date, set something so your goal is more specific)

2. Write down how the goal makes you feel

Take the time to sit down for a few minutes and engross yourself in your goal. Think about it deeply and imagine what it would be like if you had already accomplished it. Not what your life would look like, though. Imagine how you would feel. Wonder, amazement, relief, even a phrase like "I can breathe finally" associated with a financial independence goal or similar is great.

Pay attention to whatever emotions arise and jot them down. Once you're done doing this, write down, in a sentence or two, how thinking about your goal makes you feel. Make sure the description is as strong and emotionally compelling as it can possibly be.

3. Read daily

Whether you keep your goal on a piece of paper in your pocket or on the wall above your desk, make sure to read it daily. As you read over your goal, along with your description of how it makes you feel, really try to engross yourself in the empowering emotions associated with it. Use that same practice of visualization that you used before, even if only for a few seconds. The idea is that you should feel energized after reading your goals and be able to use that energy to overcome the pain of taking action (be it fear, discomfort, or other).

By utilizing this simple exercise, you'll be able to consistently generate a more pure, resilient motivation for your long-term goals that helps you overcome the immediate pain of taking action in your daily life – whether it's the fear of what someone will say or think of you, or stepping outside your comfort zone.

Lastly, give yourself credit.
It can be challenging to come up with things that you you did well. When you're just starting, you may feel like you're searching for a needle in a haystack.
Here's the good news. The more you practice it, the easier and more automatic the habit becomes. Giving yourself credit is a muscle and it strengthens with practice.

So here's a recap on strategies and activities that have the potential to revolutionize your morning routine:

1. Wake up earlier: Start your day by waking up earlier to give yourself extra time for self-care and to set a positive tone for the day.

2. Set intentions: Take a few moments each morning to set intentions for the day. Reflect on what you want to achieve and how you want to feel throughout the day.

3. Hydrate: Begin your day by drinking a glass of water to rehydrate your body and kickstart your metabolism.

4. Meditation or mindfulness: Practice meditation or mindfulness exercises to help calm your mind, reduce stress, and improve focus and clarity for the day ahead.

5. Stretch or exercise: Engage in light stretching or a short exercise routine, such as yoga or a quick workout, to wake up your body, increase energy levels, and boost your mood.

6. Gratitude practice: Take a few moments to express gratitude for the things you appreciate in your life. This practice can help shift your mindset to a positive and grateful state.

7. Healthy breakfast: Prioritize a nutritious breakfast that includes protein, whole grains, and fruits or vegetables. This will provide you with sustained energy for the day and support your overall well-being.

8. Prioritize essential tasks: Identify the most important tasks or goals for the day and focus on completing them in the morning when your energy and focus are typically higher.

9. Limit screen time: Avoid checking emails or social media first thing in the morning to protect your mental space and prevent distractions. Give yourself some screen-free time to start the day on a calmer note.

10. Practice self-care: Incorporate activities that nurture your physical, mental, and emotional well-being, such as reading, journaling, taking a relaxing bath, or listening to uplifting music.

11. Plan your day: Take a few minutes to plan out your day, review your to-do list, and prioritize your tasks. This will help you stay organized and focused on your goals.

12. Connect with loved ones: Reach out to your family, friends, or loved ones and have a meaningful conversation, send a thoughtful message, or express your love and appreciation for them.

Remember, not all strategies will work for everyone, so it's important to experiment and find what resonates with you and improves your morning routine.

A NOTE FROM THE AUTHOR

At the age of 64, I found myself embracing a new journey that would forever change my perspective on life.

One morning, I woke up feeling a sense of restlessness deep within my soul. Tired of the monotony of my daily routine, I yearned for something more fulfilling. It was then that I stumbled upon an article about the benefits of starting one's day early. Intrigued by the notion of experiencing the early morning tranquility, I decided to give it a try.

The following day, as the clock struck 4:30 am, I emerged from my slumber, feeling an unfamiliar excitement bubbling inside. I opened the curtains to witness the world still enshrouded in darkness, with faint whispers of dawn peeking through the horizon. This magical moment, where the world was just rousing from its deep slumber, filled me with a profound sense of serenity.

With newfound enthusiasm, I ventured outside, embracing the coolness of the early morning air. As I strolled through my garden every breath filled my lungs with a revitalizing energy, as if the universe itself was rejuvenating my from within. Surrounded by the stillness of the morning, my mind grew clear and focused, ready to tackle the challenges ahead.

The decision to seize the early hours not only invigorated my senses but also provided me with uninterrupted solace to ignite my creativity. Armed with a pen and notebook, I found myself effortlessly pouring out my thoughts onto the pages, creating new blogs. The silence allowed my imagination to soar, and also my book writing began to flourish.

As the days turned into weeks, I relished in the astonishing benefits of this newfound routine. Not only did I feel more organized and productive, but my body also responded positively to my early morning adventures. Physical ailments gradually diminished, replaced by a newfound vigor and vitality. My heart filled with gratitude for this simple yet transformative change I had made in my life.

It's never too late to experience the joys of a new beginning. The early morning air and stillness has rekindled my spirit, allowing me to seize each day with renewed vigor. The health benefits were just an added bonus in the grand tapestry of my life's transformation.

So, my friends, regardless of your age, I highly recommend embracing an early morning routine. In the serenity of the dawn, you may find the magic that will awaken your soul, reorganize your thoughts, and bring you closer to a feeling of being truly alive. The enormous health benefits and increased sense of well-being that accompany this routine will be the icing on the cake. Embrace the change, and let the beauty of the early morning light guide you towards a new chapter of your life.

ACKNOWLEDGMENTS

This section of the book, though seemingly challenging, is the most heartfelt and gratifying piece to write. It is a tribute to the countless individuals who have contributed to the journey of bringing this book to life. It is with profound gratitude that I express my deepest appreciation to each and every person who has touched my life and made this endeavor a reality.

First and foremost, I want to express my heartfelt gratitude to my family. Their unwavering support, love, and encouragement have been the bedrock of my journey. Their belief in me and my dreams have given me the strength to overcome obstacles and pursue my passion for writing. I am eternally grateful for their patience and understanding during the countless hours I spent lost in the world of words.

I would like to extend my deepest thanks to my mentors, both past and present, who have guided and shaped me as a person and a writer. Their wisdom, knowledge, and critique have been invaluable in refining my skills and pushing me to new heights. I am indebted to them for their continued belief in my abilities and their unyielding support.

To my friends, thank you for being the pillars of support throughout this writing journey. Your enthusiasm, encouragement, and constructive feedback have been instrumental in shaping the book. Your presence in my life has brought immense joy and comfort, and I am grateful for the countless conversations and laughter we have shared along the way.

I would also like to acknowledge the editors and proofreaders, who have contributed their expertise and skills to make this book shine. Their dedication, attention to detail, and passion for the written word have added immeasurable value to the final product. Without their time and effort, this book would not have reached its full potential.

A special mention goes to the readers and fans who have supported me throughout this journey. Your unwavering belief in my work and your enthusiasm for my works have been a constant source of inspiration. Your feedback and reviews have spurred me on during moments of doubt and reminded me of the power of writing.

Lastly, but certainly not least, I want to express my deepest gratitude to the readers of this book. Your willingness to embark on this journey with me, to open its pages and immerse yourself in its world, is an honor beyond words. It is for you that this book was written, and I hope it touches your heart, sparks your imagination, and leaves a lasting impact.

Writing this book has been a labor of love, trial, and growth. While it may have been challenging at times, the support and encouragement I have received from those around me have made all the difference. To everyone who has played a role, big or small, in the creation of this book, please accept my sincerest appreciation and gratitude. Your belief in me and this project has meant the world, and I am forever thankful for your presence in my life.

ABOUT THE AUTHOR

Stephen Cartledge is a living testament to the power of resilience and determination. His life's journey has been one of overcoming seemingly insurmountable obstacles to create a life that many would deem impossible. From his humble beginnings, living rough on the streets of Europe, to his accomplishment of building four successful bars and restaurant empires in Fuerteventura, and eventually retiring in his dream home in Thailand, Stephen's story is one of courage and unfaltering belief in the pursuit of his dreams.

Born in Dover, England, before moving to Sheffield at a young age, Stephen faced numerous challenges and setbacks early on in his life. But instead of succumbing to the hardships, he embraced them as opportunities for growth and transformation. Through sheer willpower and a relentless drive to change his circumstances, he embarked on a journey that would rewrite the trajectory of his life.

After enduring a period of homelessness in Europe, Stephen's determination led him to establish a business empire in Fuerteventura. Through hard work, dedication, and a keen entrepreneurial spirit, he transformed his circumstances, building a thriving bar and restaurant empire and becoming a respected figure in the local community.

Stephen's story is not just one of financial success, but also of personal growth and discovery. Along his journey, he learned the value of resilience, adaptability, and the importance of pursuing one's true passions. His experiences taught him that there are no limits to what one can achieve when they embrace their inner strength and refuse to be defined by their past.

Today, Stephen resides in his dream home in Thailand, basking in the fulfillment of a life well-lived. Retired from his business ventures, he continues to inspire others through his story, sharing his experiences and wisdom to help others overcome their own obstacles and create the life they desire.

Stephen's journey serves as a reminder that no matter where we come from or what challenges we face, we all have the ability to rewrite our stories and live the life of our dreams. His resilience, determination, and unwavering belief in himself are a testament to the power of the human spirit and the limitless potential within us all.

You can find the W.I.N.N.E.R Routine activities on our Facebook group. Join at:ww.riseandshinemorningglory.com

Milton Keynes UK
Ingram Content Group UK Ltd.
UKHW030416170224
437973UK00013B/1425